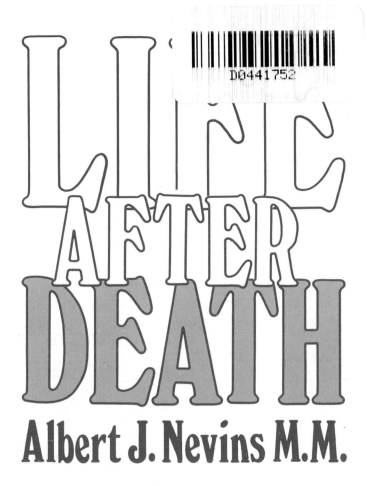

LIFE
AFTER
DEATH

Albert J. Nevins M.M.

Our Sunday Visitor, Inc.
Huntington, Indiana 46750

Nihil Obstat:
Rev. John M. Kuzmich
Censor Librorum

Imprimatur:
✠William E. McManus, D.D.
Bishop of Fort Wayne-South Bend
August 14, 1983

The Nihil Obstat and Imprimatur are official declarations that a book or pamphlet is free of doctrinal or moral error. No implication is contained therein that those who have granted the Nihil Obstat or Imprimatur agree with the contents, opinions or statements expressed.

Library of Congress Catalog Card No.: 83-61888
ISBN: 0-87973-612-7

Printed in the United States of America

Contents

CHAPTER 1

'. . . And be happy with Him forever in the next'

DEATH IS NOT A POPULAR SUBJECT. Most of us do not even like to talk about it. It takes the "touched" spirit like Peter Pan to exclaim: "To die will be an awfully big adventure!" It requires a saint like Francis of Assisi to stretch out his arms to embrace one he calls "Sister Death." It needs an optimistic philosopher like Socrates to condition his own certain fate by opining, "Death may be the greatest of all human blessings."

The modern trend is to disguise death. We speak of a deceased person as one who has "passed away." We also put "to sleep" a diseased dog. The abortion controversy has given us new terminology for death, calling the killing of the fetus "a woman's right to her body," or "termination of pregnancy," or "pro-choice action." We talk of a person's departure, or release, or eternal rest. The word "death," however, is one that most prefer to eschew.

Even in the theater where deathbed scenes were once the meat of Shakespeare's genius and the climax of grand opera, modern authors avoid them as too disturbing to the audience. Indeed, the only such scenes in modern theater that come to memory are the powerful deathbed reconciliation of the straying father in *Brideshead Revisited* and the tragic ending of *West Side Story*, which perhaps does not count as it was an update of *Romeo and Juliet*.

There even seems to be an unwritten rule that death and the afterlife are subjects to be avoided in modern preaching. Once they were the keystones of the parish mission, but ask any Catholic when was the last time he or she heard a sermon on death or heaven or hell, and the answer will be — no one remembers. These subjects seem to be as taboo as fire and brimstone. It makes some priests as uncomfortable to talk about the subjects as it does for their listeners to hear them.

The fact is that few of us are at peace with the inevitability of death. It creates an unease in us because death denies values we hold dear. Death wipes out the pleasures of the world. Death destroys riches. Death seems to end the relationships we cherish. It is an admission that we are not "masters of our fate and captains of our souls." It means leaving behind values we have chosen. As one elderly lady put it, "I don't know what I will do in heaven without television."

Our dissociation with death began with a commitment to our consumer society. In days not too far past people died in their homes and were waked in their homes. Now we move our aged to institutions, our ill to hospitals, and our corpses to resting rooms. This removes the reality and proximity of death from everyday living. The mortician picks up the body and makes the necessary cosmetic changes so that we do not even have to look on the face of death, creating the impression that the deceased is only sleeping. "She looks so beautiful, so peaceful," is the type of remark we expect to hear at the funeral home.

Consumerism also has created a society in which the concern is the here and now. Its values are of the moment. "Your economic upswing starts now," the bankers tell us as they try to lure us to their percentages of return. "You need this value! You need this price! You need this car!" shouts the auto salesman. "Isn't it worth two minutes a day to fade away age spots?" asks the beauty advertisement. On and on, day after day, from radio, television, in the press, we are assailed with things of the moment. Few ever escape the constant pressure for immediate worldly concerns.

These values even pass over into our religion. We become more caught up with social issues than eternal verities. Peace and justice are the modern watchwords, yet they too concern the here and now. Unfortunately the attempt to build a better world for today without consideration of the world to come can only result in frustration and disillusionment. We simply do not have here a lasting city, but few of us are willing to admit that fact. We build the world of tomorrow in an atomic age in which that tomorrow may never come. We dance to modern pipers, unwilling to hear the dirge of reality.

What the Christian must realize is that death and the afterlife are essential to Christian faith. They give it meaning. As St. Paul tells us: "If Christ has not been raised, our preaching is void of content and your faith is empty, too. . . . Why? Because if the dead are not raised, then Christ was not raised; and if Christ was not raised, your faith is worthless. You are still in your sins, and those who have fallen asleep in Christ are the deadest of the dead. If our hopes in Christ are limited to this life only, we are the most pitiable of men" (1 Cor 15:14, 16-19).

For the worldling, life is an end in itself. "Eat, drink and be merry for tomorrow we die," was the pagan philosophy of ancient Rome. It is still the philosophy of worldlings. For the Christian, however, the present life is but a preparation for what is to come. "In my end is my beginning," the soon-to-be executed Mary, Queen of Scots, could write. There is the certainty here of faith, a blessedness that modern agnostics deny to themselves.

Agnosticism is the intellectual disease of modern times. The tragedy is not that the agnostic does not know but that he or she does not take the time or trouble to find out. To call oneself an agnostic — to say that God's existence cannot be logically proved or disproved — is simply to boast of one's ignorance. No agnostics admit to their sickness, yet most disguise it under other names. Intellectuals cloak it under rationalism. Literati garb it in the wraps of existentialism. The so-called progressive Christians dress it up as modernism. The heresy of the agnostic is an ancient one — a desire for nothingness because the human person is helpless, thrown into a meaningless world which must tremblingly move forward to uncertain goals. Providence is a non-word.

Without an afterlife, the agnostic is right and life is meaningless, "a tale told by an idiot, full of sound and fury, signifying nothing." Life, according to George Santayana, is an interval between birth and death which is to be enjoyed. But for the saints it is a different story. St. Augustine wrote that "the sole purpose for life in time is to gain merit for life eternal." Thus for the believer everything is measured by the standard of the future rather than the present. Why? "It is no small matter to lose or gain the kingdom of heaven," Thomas à Kempis answers. For St. Francis de Sales, the world is only peopled in order that heaven may be peopled. "Thou made us for thyself, O Lord," declared St. Augustine, "and our hearts are restless until they find rest in Thee!"

When Jesus spoke of life, He did not mean the life of human days but life in eternity: "How narrow is the gate that leads to life, how rough the road, and how few there are who find it!" (Mt 7:14). Again, "Better to enter life with one eye, than to be thrown with both into fiery Gehenna" (Mt 18:9). On another occasion He told a young man seeking perfection, "If you wish to enter into life, keep the commandments" (Mt 19:17). For the Christian, then, what we call life is but a foretaste of true life which has no ending. "Methinks I am turning into a god!" the Emperor Vespasian exclaimed on his deathbed. For the Christian whose novitiate of temporal life has been a success, Vespasian was not too far from the truth.

Time is God's plan for giving us the opportunity to know and serve Him. The "penny catechism," which every child once knew by heart, succinctly answered the question of why God made mankind: "God made me to know Him, to love Him and serve Him in this world and to be happy with Him in the next." Thus the Christian measures this world with the standards of the next. What is useful to us is only that which serves eternal life, from which no one will be excluded except through one's own fault.

Catholic doctrine on this matter was summed up in 1979 in a document issued by the Sacred Congregation for the Doctrine of the Faith:

"The Church affirms that a spiritual element survives and subsists after death, an element endowed with consciousness and will, so that the 'human self' subsists. To designate this element, the Church uses the word 'soul,' the accepted term in usage of Scripture and Tradition. . . .

"In fidelity to the New Testament and Tradition, the Church believes in the happiness of the just who will one day be with Christ. She believes that there will be eternal punishment for the sinner, who will be deprived of the sight of God, and that this punishment will have a repercussion on the whole being of the sinner. She believes in the possibility of a purification for the elect before they see God, a purification altogether different from the punishment of the damned. This is what the Church means when speaking of hell and purgatory."

The afterlife is essential to Christian belief and theology. When Jesus told His followers, "I am the resurrection and the life" (Jn 11:25), He was referring to eternal life. It was to prove the existence of this eternal life that Christ rose from the dead. As Pope Paul VI said: "The Lord's resurrection is not an isolated fact, it is a fact that concerns the whole of mankind; from Christ it extends to the world; it has a cosmic importance. . . . It is on the reality of Christ's resurrection that the religion that takes its name and life from Him is founded."

Without an afterlife, present life would have no meaning. We would find ourselves like Macbeth "a walking shadow, a poor player that struts and frets his hour upon the stage and then is heard no more: it is a tale told by an idiot, full of sound and fury, signifying nothing." For the skeptical like Santayana, who held that the interval between birth and death is meaning-less and something for which there is no cure, life nec-essarily becomes something to be enjoyed as an end in itself.

Those who look upon human life as an end in itself must of necessity wind up in futility. "There is nothing left for me to do," wrote George Eastman, founder of Eastman Kodak, before he went up to his bedroom and blew his brains out. To live without God is to live with-out hope. When the only meaning of life is pleasure, or money, or power, once these things are gained or lost, there are no other worlds left. Thus we get a suicidal Eastman or an Adolf Hitler shooting himself amid the ruins of Berlin. Without belief in an afterlife, present life is hopeless — "an intolerable burden," as Mark Twain once put it. "I think, therefore I am," the phi-losopher René Descartes opined. The Christian might put it a different way: "I believe, therefore I always will be."

CHAPTER 2

The Logic of Afterlife

NEWS REPORTS CITED THE DISCOVERY
of Ice Age Texans, a man and a boy, buried in a cave.
With the bodies were beads and food, currency and
sustenance for the next world. The find is one more
proof that belief in the afterlife extends far beyond the
ancient Romans and Greeks. It seems to be a fairly
universal belief of mankind as far back as
archaeological and anthropological history can take
us. Funeral rites in the Paleolithic Age included pro-
visions of food and arms for the deceased to use in the
next life. Similarly the cult of ancestors is lost only in
prehistory. In some Paleolithic cultures even servants
or family members were slain to accompany the deceased on the voyage beyond.

The ancient Egyptians developed the coffin to preserve the body for the next life. They introduced embalming to save the corpse from corruption, and also
placed with the body familiar personal objects so that
the deceased would not be lonely in the future world.
As far back as Chinese history can be traced, there
was ancestor worship — honor given to deceased
members of the family who existed in another world.

Buddhism had its higher heavens, Judaism its nether-world of *sheol*, and Islam its heaven of flowing springs, tents with couches of thick brocade, and dark-eyed virgins "whom neither man nor genie will have touched before."

The ancient peoples of the Americas had the same type of beliefs, burying their dead with utensils they would need in the next life. The Nahuatlan poet could sing:

> We came only to be born.
> Our home is beyond:
> In the realm of the defleshed ones.

In Aztec literature that still remains we find the thought repeated that earth is "not the place of reality" but one must go beyond this life to find the realm of true happiness. As one Aztec poet put it:

> Beyond is the place where one lives.
> I would be lying to myself were I to say,
> "Perhaps everything ends on this earth;
> here do our lives end."

In ancient China, long before the birth of Christ, General Su Wu wrote his wife his belief in the here-after: "Know that if I live, I will come back again, and if I die, we will go on thinking of each other."

Thus the idea of an afterlife is not new but has ex-isted as far back as any type of record can be found. It has been found in simple cultures and complex socie-ties. Often caught up in superstition and sometimes badly distorted, it does show a continuing belief of hu-manity that life does not end with death. The idea of afterlife is a key element in understanding the major religions existing today.

Basic to belief in an afterlife is the fundamental conviction about the existence of the soul — that spiritual element of the person which continues to endure after bodily death. While there may be differences in concepts about the nature of the soul, and the mode of future existence of the soul, there is a general belief that there exists a spiritual principle that goes on after death.

In Islam, according to the Koran, "each soul is the hostage to its own deeds." The soul is the spirit God breathed into Adam and into each person born. After death the souls of the pious stay near Allah to be reunited with the body on Judgment Day; the souls of the impious are condemned to the fires of hell. Over the centuries a rather elaborate eschatology, or belief in the last things, has developed but the basic belief of Muhammad has changed little. The heaven and hell of Islam are described in material terms that are very real to believers of the Prophet.

Hinduism has no founder but is a body of beliefs developed over 4,000 years. It is best described as an ancient synthesis of religions. There is a world soul (brahman) with which the individual soul (atman) is identified. Death does not mean final union with God. According to the doctrine of *karma*, the individual can go through a series of lifetimes (reincarnation) which will only end through the elimination of the passions and an understanding of reality. When that point is reached, final union with God takes place. Modern Hinduism is split into many sects, some heretical; one school (Charvaka) even rejects the idea of *karma*, holding there is no God or future life. However, basic to heterodox Hinduism are the concepts and relationships of God, world and soul.

There is a similarity to Hinduism in Buddhism. Central to Buddhist doctrine are the tenets that existence is suffering, and suffering is caused by craving and attachment. The ideal is the perfected saint who is purified of all attachments and desires. To reach this state one may have to go through a series of births and rebirths until the ultimate purification attains the total transcendence of nirvana. There are various Buddhist sects, but the basic teaching is common to all, and monasteries, where the purification can be lived so that the soul will be freed, are found throughout Buddhist lands.

One of the most prevalent and enduring religions of the world is that of animism, which is totally unorganized and which exists among primitive people on tribal levels. It was largely the religion of the American Indians. Animism is the belief that within every material object there is a soul which gives its existence. This spirit is eternal. There is a spirit world of good and bad spirits, of major and lesser gods. Some tribes are monotheistic, but pantheism is more common.

Arising from animism is the religion of ancestor worship, which became a major force in China, Japan, Africa, and on the islands of the South Pacific. This is a belief that the souls (spirits) of the dead continue to inhabit the material world and can influence the fate of the living. These spirits must be propitiated and honored. Practice of ancestor worship includes home altars to the dead, bringing gifts of food to the graves of the deceased, passing on the names of the deceased to the living, and so on.

The point of all this is to show that there is and has always been a great universal consent to the ideas of soul and afterlife. The deathlessness of the soul has been a consistent belief of most of mankind. Although details of the afterlife may differ in East and West, and between religions and sects of the same religion, there is a common belief that each individual has a soul which lives on beyond the body.

The Christian explanation for these widespread beliefs is that they are all part of God's revelation to man, often distorted by time, distance and culture, yet going back to a common source and tradition.

CHAPTER 3

Afterlife in the Old Testament

THE JEWISH COSMOLOGY
of the Old Testament was very simplistic and
primitive, differing little from that of the Jew's non-
covenant neighbors. The earth was conceived as a
platform resting on columns that reached down into an
abyss. Where these columns rose above the earth, they
became mountains. Surrounding the earth and going
down into the abyss were the seas and oceans. Above
the earth was the firmament which contained the sun,
moon, and stars, bounded in a great arc by some type
of wall, reaching from one end of the earth to the other, and broken only by floodgates. Outside the wall
were waters which would be released through the
floodgates from time to time, letting down rain and
snow upon the earth. Above the waters was heaven,
the seat of the divinity.

Deep within the bowels of the earth was a place
called *sheol*, the abode of the dead. It was a region of
thick darkness and gloom (Job 10:21), deep down (Job
11:8), full of dust (Job 17:16), hidden (Job 14:13), a
place of no return (Job 10:21), a gathering place for all
the living (Job 30:23). It was a place of neither punish-

ment nor reward; a rendezvous for kings and counselors, slaves and free, wicked and good, weary and infants (Job 3:13-19). He who went down to sheol would not come up again. Sheol was a vast tomb where the dead lay inert. As the *Jerome Commentary* puts it: "Sheol is not a form of survival but a denial of survival." Death was the termination of life, and there was no idea of escape. Even the Psalmist (9:14) saw sheol as a prison house with gates.

As Jewish thought developed, however, various writers began wrestling with the problem of death. The Psalmist in various places opines that there must be some reward for virtue, otherwise wickedness and virtue would have the same results. Qoheleth (Ecclesiastes) puzzles over the meaning of death in chapters 8 and 9, and concludes man does not know the future. Sirach pondered the same problem and decided the wicked would receive retribution in this world, particularly in the last hours (11:26-28), while the virtuous would die peacefully.

By the time of Enoch, ideas on death had begun to change. While the Books of Enoch are not canonical by either Jewish or Catholic standards, the writings do show the ideas of the age in which they were written. In 1 Enoch, the oldest, sheol has moved closer to the modern concept of hell. It is no longer a place of extinction, and although the good and bad are together in hell (22), the bad suffer while the good are happy. The Book of Wisdom differentiated between spiritual and physical death, suggesting that the latter was suffered only by the wicked "for righteousness is immortal" (1:15 — RSV).

Much of the Jewish difficulty arose because of an imperfect knowledge of the soul — a breath breathed into Adam by God. In Greek philosophy, which greatly influenced the New Testament, man was an incarnate spirit; the preexistent soul is actually sullied by contact with the body and seeks deliverance through death. In the Greek view, the soul is the main element of the person; the body is something tacked on but not essential to being. The Jewish view, on the other hand, was the exact opposite. It was the body which was formed first, with life breathed into it by God. For the Greeks, thought was a spiritual process. For the Jews, the heart was the organ of thought, not the mind or some spiritual principle.

Jewish opinion, therefore, focused on the body and not on the soul. The Jews knew the body died, and thus it seemed with death all was ended. Yet the Psalmist was troubled. Such an end befitted the ungodly, but Psalm 49:16 expresses the hope that for the just "God will redeem me from the power of the nether world by receiving me." This view was even clearer to the author of Psalm 73, who concluded that while the wicked prospered in this life and the just seemed to suffer in vain, the only solution to the imbalance of justice is in the hereafter when the wicked will be punished and the good will enjoy the presence of God forever. Thus in Jewish literature, hope was beginning to appear, but it was vague and formless.

Then into Jewish spiritual thought came the idea of resurrection as the culmination of the Psalmist's hope. Isaiah (26:19) expressed that hope exuberantly: "But the dead shall live, their corpses shall rise; awake and sing, you who lie in the dust." This revelation of the prophet was perhaps the background for Daniel's belief in new life (12:2): "Many of those who sleep in the dust of the earth shall awake; some shall live forever, others shall be an everlasting horror and disgrace.''

By the time of the Maccabees (second century before Christ), belief in existence after death and the ability of the living to aid the dead had become accepted ideas. The mother of the martyred sons exhorts the youngest to be worthy of his faith so that the family will be together again after death. The young boy dies in confidence of a "never-failing life" (2 Macc 7:36). Later Judas Maccabeus takes up a collection to provide an expiatory sacrifice for his fallen soldiers. The author makes his own commentary on this act: "In doing this he acted in a very excellent and noble way, inasmuch as he had the resurrection of the dead in view; for if he were not expecting the fallen to rise again, it would have been useless and foolish to pray for them in death" (2 Macc 12:39-46).

The idea of an afterlife came to fruition in Wisdom, the last book of the Old Testament. Wisdom stresses continued life with God, based not so much on the Greek concept of an immortal soul as on the nature of God's relationship with humanity, which "fashioned all things that they might have being." God does not even will death nor rejoice in the destruction of the living; death is the result of sin (Wis 1:13-16). While there is no mention of the resurrection of the body in Wisdom, the idea of afterlife is thematic to the book, which became an excellent preparation for the teachings of Christ.

Like Wisdom, the Qumran documents (Dead Sea Scrolls) show a belief in afterlife, but so far there has been no document found concerned with resurrection of the body. However, by the time of Christ this subject was often under bitter debate. Although the

Pharisees represented the majority opinion upholding immortality and resurrection, the less numerous sect of Sadducees denied immortality, the resurrection and the existence of angels. The conservative Sadducees accepted only the Law as the basis for Judaism, and since the Law said nothing about resurrection, the Sadducees denied it. Both John the Baptist and Christ were critical of the Sadducees.

There is indirect evidence also in the Old Testament of a belief in the afterlife. Elijah going off to heaven in a chariot of fire was not bound for sheol but life with God. Malachi (3:23) prophesied that Elijah would return again to earth before the end of the world. In Ezekiel, chapter 37, the prophet has a vision of dry bones coming together and returning to life. As the Lord God says to Ezekiel: "You shall know that I am the Lord, when I open your graves and have you rise from them" (Ezek 37:13).

Finally, there are other apocrypha besides Enoch which, while not inspired, show beliefs of their time. The Psalms of Solomon and the Book of Jubilees indicate belief in an afterlife and in resurrection. Thus, while the early books of the Old Testament may be labeled "non-eschatological," later inspired writings and other Jewish literature show the development of belief in the afterlife and then hope in a resurrection.

More modern Jewish thinking is expressed by that teacher of Scripture Maimonides (Rabbi Moses ben Maimon, 1134-1204), who taught that the soul comes directly from God, and that once created it is never destroyed because it does not require physical life for its activities. A good life brings a reward to the righteous in the world to come, a life that is marked by goodness and happiness. As Maimonides, a philosher, wrote in his *Commentary to Mishna: Sanhedrin*: "I believe with perfect faith that there will be a revival of the dead at the time when it shall please the Creator."

This teaching of Maimonides is the prevalent thought in the mainstream of Jewish life today. In Reformed Judaism the afterlife is not considered a necessary doctrine and adherents are left to believe or disbelieve as they choose. However, even among those who are uncertain of an afterlife, there is a vicarious immortality in their children. The memory of the deceased is honored, and children are given their names, as if in this manner the ancestors' existence could be continued.

CHAPTER 4

Afterlife in the New Testament and the Apostolic Church

"SCIENCE DENIES IMMORTALITY,"
shouted the headline on one of those sensational news-papers one finds at the check-out lanes of the super-market. It had been undoubtedly placed there to pique the curiosity of the passerby, although it shouldn't have because the story inside had to be untrue and without substance. Science can neither deny nor af-firm immortality. Science is concerned with natural laws, and immortality is beyond nature. Science deals with the physical, namely, that which can be meas-ured. The metaphysical does not belong to science. If the headline had read "Scientists Deny Immortality," it would have made sense. But the response would have been similar to the real headline: "So what? Im-mortality is not the province of scientists."

Immortality pertains to theology and religion. It presumes a belief in God, and this belief in God leads to one of the philosophical arguments for immortality. Unless we are willing to affirm that God is unjust (and that would bring crashing down the whole structure of theology), we must affirm His justice. Since justice is

19

too seldom present in this world, there must be a time and place where each will receive according to his or her deeds. This has to be an afterlife.

St. Irenaeus (ca. 130-200), one of the Fathers of the early Church, had another argument. He wrote to the Christians of his time: "Why should you not believe that you will exist again after this life? Is it harder for God who made your body when it was not to make it anew when it has been?" St. Thomas Aquinas found another proof in the consistent belief of mankind: "The conviction that faith brings with it eternal life, that is to say, the divine life of God Himself, sums up the accumulated experience of centuries."

The central theme of the New Testament is eternal life — the immortality of the Christian sharing in the resurrection of Christ. In the New Testament eternal life is a reality, a gift of Jesus which at the same time must be earned. Jesus began His mission by appearing in Galilee with the rallying cry: "Reform your lives: The kingdom of heaven is at hand" (Mt 4:17). The kingdom of heaven was to be an endless reign of eternal life.

Early in His mission apostolate, Jesus received under the cover of darkness a member of the Sanhedrin, Nicodemus the Pharisee. In explaining Himself, Jesus said: "Yes, God so loved the world that he gave his only Son, that whoever believes in him may not die but may have eternal life" (Jn 3:16). It was a theme Jesus was to repeat over and over. In His discourse on the Bread of Life, Jesus told the crowd of Jews: "Indeed, this is the will of my Father, that everyone who looks upon the Son and believes in him shall have eternal life. Him I will raise up on the last day" (Jn 6:40). Even before Jesus began His ministry, John the Baptist had given similar testimony about Him: "Whoever believes in the Son has life eternal. . ." (Jn 3:36).

In His discourse on Sabbath work, Jesus told His critics that belief in the Scriptures was not enough for salvation. He challenged them: "Search the Scriptures in which you think you have eternal life — they also testify on my behalf. Yet you are unwilling to come to me to possess that life" (Jn 5:39-40). To the Samaritan woman at the well in Shechem Jesus promised that the water He could give her would "provide eternal life" (Jn 4:14). Membership in the kingdom that Jesus was founding ensured immortality. On the feast of Dedication, Jesus was at the Temple in Solomon's Portico, and He told the Jews there: "My sheep hear my voice. I know them and they follow me. I give them eternal life and they shall never perish. No one shall snatch them out of my hand" (Jn 10:27-28).

On occasion Jesus conditioned His remarks on eternal life. Speaking once to Philip and Andrew (Jn 12:25), Jesus said: "The man who loves his life loses it, while the man who hates his life in this world preserves it to life eternal." Another time Jesus told His disciples that eternal life was a reward for their sacrifices: "Everyone who has given up home, brothers or sisters, father or mother, wife or children, or property for my sake will receive many times as much and inherit everlasting life" (Mt 19:29). The Eucharist was also made a condition (Jn 6:54): "He who feeds on my flesh and drinks my blood has life eternal, and I will raise him up on the last day."

In short, His message was brief: "He who believes has eternal life" (Jn 6:47). That His Apostles understood the message is also clear. After His revelation of the Eucharist many disciples turned away from Him because the teaching was more than they could accept. Jesus asked His Apostles if they also would go. Peter spoke for all: "Lord, to whom should we go? You have the words of eternal life" (Jn 6:68).

The theme of everlasting life through belief in Jesus was the foundation of apostolic preaching. The Book of Acts (13:46) related how Paul and Barnabas told the dissenters that it was the will of God that the Good News should first be preached to them, but since they rejected it they thus "convict (themselves) as unworthy of everlasting life." The gentiles delighted in this decision to turn the mission to themselves and "all who were destined to life everlasting believed in it" (Acts 13:48).

Paul made immortality an important point in his own teaching. He told the Galatians (6:8) that the "fruit of the spirit is everlasting life." To the Romans he wrote (6:23): "The wages of sin is death, but the gift of God is eternal life in Christ Jesus our Lord." He exhorts Timothy not to risk losing eternal life: "Fight the good fight of faith. Take firm hold on the everlasting life to which you were called, when in the presence of many witnesses, you made your noble profession of faith" (1 Tim 6:12). This reference is to Timothy's baptism and the profession of faith made on that occasion.

For John the matter was very simple. His Gospel is replete with references to eternal life, mainly in the words of Christ Himself. Thus in an Epistle (1 Jn 2:25) he would sum it up simply: "He himself made us a promise and the promise is no less than this: eternal life."

Eternal life was the ever-present goal of the Christians of apostolic times. Martyrdom for the new faith was never remote, yet at the same time never feared, since it was the gateway to that eternal life. This explains why the martyrs went to their deaths singing. St. Ignatius, head of the Church at Antioch, was apprehended by Roman authorities and condemned to death (A.D. 108). On his way to execution he wrote a last letter to his Christian community, begging the Christians not to interfere. "Suffer me to be eaten by the beasts, through whom I can attain to God," he wrote. "I am God's wheat, and I am ground by the teeth of wild beasts that I may be found pure bread of Christ. Rather entice the wild beasts that they may become my tomb. . . . If I suffer I shall be Jesus Christ's freedman, and in him shall I rise free."

Ancient writings, while not canonical, attest to the concern of the early Christians with eternal life. The *Didache*, or *Teaching of the Twelve Apostles*, concludes with an announcement of the resurrection on the last day. The Epistle of Barnabas, although apocryphal, promises, "Whoever believes in Him shall live forever." In fact, the whole Epistle is concerned with those things "bearing on salvation." It concludes with the admonition: "Surely, whoever complies with [the demands of the Lord] will reap glory in the kingdom of God; whoever chooses the opposite course with all its works must perish. That is why there is a resurrection, why there is a retribution."

St. Polycarp, Bishop of Smyrna, was a contemporary of St. Ignatius and himself a martyr in A.D. 155 or 156. In his Epistle to the Philippians, Polycarp promised, "He who has raised Him from the dead will raise us also, provided we do His will." In another place in the Epistle he warns that "whoever wrests the Lord's Gospel to suit his own lusts and denies both resurrection and judgment — such a one is the first-born of Satan.''

When he was an old man, over one hundred years, Polycarp was arrested by Roman authorities and condemned to death. *The Martyrdom of Polycarp*, an eyewitness account of the events around the martyrdom, by a Christian named Marcion, was sent to the Christians worldwide. When Polycarp was led into the arena, he was made to stand before the Roman proconsul, who sought to mitigate the punishment due the old man by inviting him to recant. When Polycarp remained firm the official threatened him with wild beasts. Polycarp said he was not afraid of wild beasts.

"If you make little of the beasts," the proconsul replied, "I shall have you consumed by fire unless you change your mind."

"The fire with which you threaten," Polycarp answered, "only burns for a little while and then goes out. You do not seem to know of the fire of the judgment to come and the eternal punishment which awaits the wicked."

Since the proconsul could not move Polycarp, he ordered that he be burned to death. As the fire was built around Polycarp, the old man prayed aloud: "I bless Thee, because Thou has seen fit to bestow upon me this day and this hour, that I may share, among the martyrs, the cup of Thy Anointed and rise to eternal life both in soul and in body, in virtue of the immortality of the Holy Spirit."

The account closes by calling Polycarp's day of martyrdom "his birthday." This is the oldest account we have which calls the day of death a birthday, indicating that the Christians regarded death as nothing more than a passage into eternal life. Ignatius of Antioch also anticipated this *dies natalis* when as he awaited his martyrdom he wrote: "The birth pangs are upon me."

Thus in the New Testament, and in the writings of the Fathers, eternal life was central to Christian belief in a far more positive and detailed way than can be found in the Old Testament. The doctrine of eternal life was one of the revolutionary teachings of the new religion, and it gave hope to both Jews and pagans who were without hope.

Finally, many of the Fathers of the early Church were strongly influenced by the Book of Revelation, which was apocalyptic in character. This was particularly true of Irenaeus, Origen, and Clement of Alexandria. This last book of the New Testament, apart from some introductory greetings to the Seven Churches, is entirely concerned with the eschatological future and closes with the new world and new Jerusalem which will exist after the universal judgment.

CHAPTER 5

'I believe . . . in the resurrection of the body, and life everlasting. Amen'

THE TITLE OF THIS CHAPTER
is taken from the closing words of the Apostles' Creed, a formula of belief that every Catholic is expected to learn at an early age. This most ancient form of the Creed, both in Western and Eastern versions, proclaims belief in the resurrection as an article of faith. The Church has consistently taught that in the consummation of the world there will be a resurrection of the dead, of all who have lived, even of the damned, which will not be purely spiritual; also, there will follow a universal judgment which will be carried out through Jesus Christ, who renders to each according to his or her works. When this is done, the Church will reign with Christ forever, nor will there by any metamorphosis of the impious.

The New Testament concept of resurrection is essentially different from the Greek idea of immortality. The Greeks envisioned a continued spiritual life for the soul which somehow after death of the body became merged in divine immortality; all ties with the body were ended. In late Old Testament theology, the soul was temporarily imprisoned in sheol while awaiting resurrection and reunion with the body. "He who maintains that the resurrection is not a biblical doctrine has no share in the world to come," declares the Jewish *Mishna: Sanhedrin*, expressing a hope of Jewish theology. "The Lord puts to death and gives life; he casts down to the nether world; he raises up again," promises 1 Samuel 2:6. Both the Prophets Elijah and Elisha worked resurrection miracles, proving that God could recall souls from sheol and reunite them with the body.

In contrasting the Greek and Christian ideas of immortality, Joseph Ratzinger observes: "Actually, what was originally involved were not two complementary notions, but rather two complete answers to the future of man. As its basis the Greek idea has the notion of two heterogeneous substances which have been added together in man, one of which decays (the body) while the other (the soul) is of itself immortal and thus able to continue existing in itself, independently of any other being; only then, in separation from its essentially alien and mortal body, is the soul able to achieve its full and proper self. In contrast to this, biblical thought presupposes an indivisible unity of man; for example, the Bible has no term which signifies only the body (separated and differentiated from the soul); vice versa the word 'soul' always means the whole man existing bodily (J. Schmid)." Ratzinger concludes that resurrection "concerns the salvation of man as one and indivisible" (*Encyclopedia of Theology*, Karl Rahner, ed., Seabury).

Karl Rahner uses an existential argument to prove the resurrection of the body. He writes: "Man is a being who looks to a future which is his fulfillment. Because man is a unity, he cannot at all events spontaneously think of this fulfillment, this goal in life, simply as a fulfillment of the 'soul,' . . . If 'flesh' in the biblical sense is understood as man's perishable being, it is quite possible to say that man turns in hope to the 'resurrection of the flesh' as the fulfillment of his existence. . . . God's self-communication to man in grace has a history directed towards such fulfillment in which the Pneuma saves and transfigures the whole man. Man is constituted as supernaturally transcendent.''

The key to the understanding of the resurrection of the body is to be found in the paschal experience, for as Paul tells us: "If Christ has not been raised, our preaching is void of content and your faith is empty too'' (1 Cor 15:14). The resurrection of Christ is made all the more real because the Apostles and disciples did not believe that a physical resurrection would take place. The death of Jesus was for them a tragic ending of a beautiful life. The holy women intended to return to the tomb to complete the burial of Jesus when the Sabbath had ended. When they did return and found an empty tomb, Mary Magdalene told Peter, ''The Lord has been taken from the tomb! We don't know where they have put him!'' (Jn 20:2). John was the only one who believed what had really happened (Jn 20:8), and even he apologizes for his fellow disciples, ''Remember, as yet they did not understand the Scripture that Jesus had to rise from the dead'' (Jn 20:9). So except for John and the enemies of Jesus, who, while they probably did not believe, decided to place a guard at the tomb so that the body could not be stolen, the actual resurrection was a non-event.

But then the risen Jesus began to make His appearances "over a period of many days" (Acts 13:31). To Paul, the resurrection of Christ was central to his teaching. In 1 Corinthians 15:5-8, he outlines the appearances: "First to Cephas (Peter), then by the Twelve. After that he was seen by five hundred brothers at once, most of whom are still alive, although some have fallen asleep. Next he was seen by James then by all the apostles. Last of all he was seen by me as one born out of normal course." The Gospels relate other appearances and further details. Jesus appeared to Mary Magdalene, to the Apostles behind locked doors, to the doubting Thomas, to the disciples in Galilee. Finally, "he led them out near Bethany, and with hands upraised blessed them. As he blessed them, he left them, and was taken up to heaven" (Lk 24:50-51).

Thus, as Paul put it, Jesus became the firstborn of the dead, a new Adam from whom all would have eternal life. He outlines his doctrine in the first Epistle to the Corinthians: "But as it is, Christ is now raised from the dead, the first fruits of those who have fallen asleep. Death came through a man; hence the resurrection of the dead comes through a man also. Just as in Adam all die, so in Christ all will come to life again, but each one in proper order: Christ the first fruits and then, at his coming, all those who belong to him. After that will come the end, when, after having destroyed every sovereignty, authority, and power, he will hand over the kingdom to God the Father. Christ must reign until God has put all enemies under his feet, and the last enemy to be destroyed is death" (15:20-26).

It was the promise of resurrection that made Paul's apostolate worth while. "If I fought those beasts at Ephesus for purely human motives, what profit was there for me?'' he asks (1 Cor 13:32). "If the dead are not raised, 'let us eat and drink, for tomorrow we die!' '' In the resurrection, Paul tells us (1 Cor 15:42-43), comes human fulfillment: "What is sown in the earth is subject to decay, what rises is incorruptible. What is sown is ignoble, what rises is glorious. Weakness is sown, strength rises up. A natural body is put down and a spiritual body comes up.'' Then at the end of his Epistle, he describes the moment of resurrection: "The trumpet will sound and the dead will be raised incorruptible, and we shall be changed. This corruptible body must be clothed with incorruptibility, this mortal body with immortality. When the corruptible frame takes on incorruptibility and the mortal immortality, then will the saying of Scripture be fulfilled: 'Death is swallowed up in victory.' 'O death, where is your victory? O death, where is your sting?' '' (1 Cor 15:52-55).

The Book of Revelation (20:11-15) also tells of the resurrection of the dead, with the earth and sea giving up their bodies, and each person being judged according to his or her conduct. Those whose names are not listed in the Book of Life kept by the Lamb are hurled into a second and unending death. But for those who will remain living there is a new Jerusalem, "beautiful as a bride.'' This will be "God's dwelling among men.'' They shall be His people and He shall be their God who is always with them. In this new Jerusalem "there shall be no more death or mourning, crying out or pain, for the former world has passed away'' (Rev 21:4). Thus the Christian waits impatiently for the day when all this will come to pass, but in his religion he already possesses the promise. The resurrection will only reveal the reality of the present mystery.

This doctrine of the New Testament is fundamental to Christian teaching. It has also been noted that the earliest Creeds make the resurrection of the body an article of faith. The Council of Toledo, which met in the year 400, affirmed belief "that there will assuredly be a resurrection of the human flesh" and the same council declared: "If anyone says and (or) believes that the human bodies will not rise again (do not rise) after death, let him be anathema" (Denzinger 30). Succeeding councils and popes have continually affirmed this basic Catholic doctrine.

St. Thomas Aquinas uses a number of arguments to justify his belief in bodily resurrection. One is based on Chapter 5 of Romans. The gift of Christ is greater than the sin of Adam. Adam's sin brought death. Christ's victory conquered death. Therefore, by the gift of Christ man will be restored from death to life. Another argument Aquinas uses is based on the doctrine of the Mystical Body. "The members should be conformed to the head," he writes in the *Summa* (Q 75, a 1 Suppl). "Now our head lives and will live eternally in body and soul; since Christ rising from the dead dieth now no more (Rom 6:8). Therefore those who are His members will live in body and soul; and consequently there must needs be a resurrection of the body." Another argument is philosophical. Man is a composite of matter and form. Since the soul is united to the body as form to matter, it takes both to give complete happiness, and so we must therefore of necessity uphold the resurrection.

An important text to Aquinas is Job 19:26: "And from my flesh I shall see God; my inmost being is consumed with longing." This desire for immortality is in itself a proof of its existence. He writes: "The necessity of holding the resurrection arises from this — that man may obtain the last end for which he was made; for this cannot be accomplished in this life, nor in the life of the separated soul; otherwise man would have been made in vain, if he were unable to attain the end for which he was made. And since it behooves the end to be obtained by the selfsame thing that was made for that end, lest it appear to be made without a purpose, it is necessary for the selfsame man to arise again; and this is effected by the selfsame soul being united to the selfsame body. For otherwise there would be no resurrection properly speaking, if man was not re-formed. Hence to maintain that he who rises again is not the selfsame man is heretical, since it is contrary to the truth of Scripture which proclaims the resurrection" (*Summa*, Q 79, a 2 Suppl).

The purpose of resurrection, therefore, is not to continue the human race but to perpetuate the individual, and the individual is both body and soul. As *The Teaching of Christ* (Lawler, Wuerl and Lawler) tells us: "Each will rise as the same person he was, in the same flesh made living by the same spirit. But life will be richly enlarged and deepened. . . . Bodily resurrection, implying the transformation of the whole man, will be the beginning and in a real sense the source of the definitive happiness of the community of believers in Christ." Because we are perpetuated as individuals, our identities do not change. This does not mean that we will be unchanged. While we will arise from the dead as the same person, we will be a vastly changed person, particularly as regards our bodies.

St. Paul indicated this change (1 Cor 15:42-44): "What is sown in the earth is subject to decay, what rises is incorruptible. What is sown is ignoble, what rises is glorious. Weakness is sown, strength rises up. A natural body is put down and a spiritual body comes up." Theologians call this risen body a "glorified body." Father John Hardon, S.J., in his *Catholic Catechism* describes it in these words: "Since the Council of Trent, four terms have been officially used to identify the qualities of the risen body: impassibility, or immunity from death and pain; subtility, or freedom from restraint by matter; agility, or obedience to spirit with relation to movement and space; and clarity, or refulgent beauty of the soul manifested in the body."

Thus although we are the same, we become different. What was mortal has become immortal. Freed from sickness and pain, spared further uncertainty and doubt, we exist forever in a blessedness and happiness that is unimaginable in our present existence.

CHAPTER 6

Death

BOB NIZZI, AN IOWA BASKETBALL COACH, was having a pregame meal before an away game when he suddenly felt a surge of pain and keeled over. He was rushed to a hospital, the apparent victim of a heart attack. An emergency medical team found his heart sound but diagnosed a perforated ulcer. He was hurried to the operating room where during a long surgery the doctors nearly lost him. When he recovered, he described the experience of near death. He says he was in a long tunnel, quiet and serene. At the end of the tunnel was a light. As he moved toward the light, he was joined by two deceased friends. As he approached, the light became brighter and brighter and more dazzling until he suddenly knew it was the light of Christ.

Tom S., a New Jersey teamster, had a similar experience. He was underneath a truck making repairs when the jack gave way and the vehicle crashed down on him. When he was finally pulled out, he was believed to be dead, but later at the hospital he was revived. In describing the experience, Tom told of finding himself in a dark tunnel, completely black, through which he was moving blindly but surely. Then he noticed a glimmer of light, and as he approached it, it became brighter and brighter, until he was engulfed in a magnificent light in which he was sure that he would find the essence of God. Before he passed through the light or understood it, he was reluctantly called back to consciousness.

Eugene Condon was 28 years old when on Long Island, New York, he accidentally touched an electric power line that sent 32,000 volts (115 amps) of electricity through him. When he was freed of the wire, however, he showed no signs of life. He describes how he watched from above his body as a doctor tried to revive him while a priest gave him last rites. He accompanied his body to the hospital and watched as he was left for removal to the morgue. A passing nurse thought she saw a glimmer of life, and he too was revived.

These three experiences are similar to many other near-death accounts which have appeared in a flood of articles in recent years. It is quite probable that not too many years ago these people would have died, but improved medical techniques have restored life to what seemed hopeless cases. This is particularly true of people who have undergone heart attacks, submersions or electrical shocks.

Dr. Michael B. Sabom, a medical professor at Emory University, Atlanta, has devoted considerable time to recording near-death experiences. His findings show that people look upon their approaching death with almost third-person clinical interest, of experiencing a great tranquillity and a desire not to return to life.

Having collected a large number of cases over his

half-dozen years of research, Dr. Sabom divides near-death experiences into three types.

• *Autoscopic.* This is like a third-person experience. The consciousness leaves the body and seems to stand at one side, aware of its surroundings and looking down on efforts being made to resuscitate the body. There is a feeling of serenity and peace.

• *Transcendental.* Here the consciousness leaves the body but does not stay to observe. It moves through a dark area toward a dazzling light into a place of great beauty where one meets, he says, "relatives, friends or a religious figure who tells them that it is not the time to be there — to return."

• *A combination of both.* The person hovers above his or her body as if attracted to it but then slowly moves off into an area of darkness. This could be an autoscopic experience on the way to a transcendental one.

One thing all of these experiences have in common, Dr. Sabom reports, is that the person involved was not pronounced clinically dead. Science has recorded no case of a person clinically dead being restored to life. Certain saints are said to have restored people to life, and there are accounts in the Gospels and Acts, but there is a question of whether all these happenings involved people who were actually dead.

There was an incident of the synagogue leader who came to Jesus and told Him his daughter was dead. Jesus arrived at a house full of mourners. But note His words: "Leave, all of you! The little girl is not dead. She is asleep" (Mt 9:24). The people did not believe Him and ridiculed Him. The Gospel tells us that Jesus "took her by the hand and she got up" (Mt 9:25). Was she really dead or only in a coma from which He aroused her? Then there was the case of the only son of the widow of Naim. He was being carried out for burial when Jesus was entering the town. Jesus stopped the cortege, saying, "Young man, I bid you get up" (Lk 7:14). Scripture reports, "The dead man sat up and began to speak" (Lk 7:15). But was he really clinically dead? It is common knowledge that before the days of embalming, people were often buried alive, and even today there are cases of people reviving while on an undertaker's slab.

Indeed, the Church in its process of canonization causes the tomb of the person under scrutiny to be opened and the body examined to see if it is as it was when buried. There must be certainty that the person did not emerge from a coma and experience the possibility of final despair.

The one case in the Gospels that cannot be so explained is the death of Lazarus, the brother of Martha and Mary. Jesus had delayed going to His friend for several days after word was sent out that he was dying. When He finally decided to go to Bethany, He told His disciples clearly, "Lazarus is dead. For your sakes, I am glad I was not there, that you may come to believe" (Jn 11:14).

When Jesus reached Bethany, Lazarus had been dead for four days. Jesus asked Mary and Martha to accompany Him to the tomb. When he asked to have the stone sealing the door rolled back, Martha protested, "There will be a stench" (Jn 11:39). (How much more graphic the old Douai-Rheims Version: "By this time he stinks!") After praying, Jesus cries out, "Lazarus, come out!" (Jn 11:43). Then in prefiguration of Jesus' own resurrection, Lazarus comes forth, the burial shroud still tightly bound around him. I am sure Dr. Sabom would give anything to have interviewed Lazarus.

For the Christian, the nature of death is clear. St. Ambrose stated it simply in the fourth century: "Death is the separation of soul and body." For science, however, the matter is not quite that simple. For many years, members of the American Medical Association and the American Bar Association have debated a definition of death. Before the age of electronics, death was assumed to have taken place when neither breath nor heartbeat could be detected. The lack of sound in a stethoscope, or the lack of fogging on a mirror held before lips and nose, or the failure to detect a pulse, indicated death.

Today, however, modern resuscitation methods can restore heartbeat and respiration to victims of drowning, heart attack, electrical shock and other accidents. Moreover, the heart and lung machine can keep lungs breathing and heart beating long after they cannot do so on their own. Fred Snite, a victim of polio paralysis, could not breathe on his own. An iron lung kept him alive for many years and enabled him to father children.

Reflex tests were also used to gauge death. Their lack, coupled with no breathing or heartbeat, indicated the cessation of life. Then came the invention of the electroencephalograph (EEG) which measures the electrical impulses of the brain. When brain waves cease to appear on the screen, death is indicated.

Death ordinarily follows a pattern. When the lungs fail, the heart gets no oxygen; when that ceases, the heart stops and fails to pass oxygen to the brain; and without oxygen the brain dies. Father Charles J. McFadden, O.S.A., whose specialty is medical ethics, sums it up this way: "Within *ten seconds* after blood circulation has ceased, consciousness will disappear; within *five minutes* the brain cells will begin to die; and within *fifteen minutes* there will be complete and permanent cessation of brain function, that is, total *brain death* will have resulted."

As a result of modern knowledge, death is now being defined as "a permanent and irreversible cessation of integrated cerebral activity, heartbeat and respiration."

But all of that is clinical and scientific jargon which leaves us uncomfortable. As pointed out at the beginning of this book, death is something most people would prefer not to talk about. Few want to dwell on its inevitability and hence do not plan for it in any practical way. People put off making wills and die in testate. Catholics hesitate about calling the priest for sacramental Anointing of the Sick. Who ever heard of children being taught about death? Yet it should be a reality of life for them. The time to prepare for death is long before the fatal illness.

How rare are people like Colonel Charles Lindbergh, the famed aviator and first man to fly solo across the Atlantic Ocean. When Colonel Lindbergh was stricken with cancer, he prepared for his own end. Hospitalized in a New York City cancer center, he was told that he had only a week or two left of life. He had himself discharged from the hospital and, with his family, enplaned to the home he loved in Maui, Hawaii. There, he called in some Hawaiian cowboys and had them build a coffin out of eucalyptus wood. He selected the work clothes in which he would be buried. On a prechosen site on a cliff overlooking the Pacific, he was buried a few hours after his death. The only prayer said over his grave was one he composed. In his dying, Charles Lindbergh was as he was in life — not afraid of the unknown; nor was he unwilling to share his passing with those whom he loved.

Those who have made a study of the process of dying have learned that few people are at peace with the issues of death. There is an almost universal psychological process which must be undergone. Dr. Elisabeth Kübler-Ross, a published authority on death and dying, defines five stages which people go through when told that they have a fatal illness.

1. Denial and isolation. This is the "No, not me" stage. They find the diagnosis hard to believe and often shop around for other opinions. They keep the news to themselves and do not want to share it with others.

2. Anger. "Why me?" stage. They take out their anger on those about them. There is a tendency to bargain with God, as if some promise that can be made will remove the sentence of death.

3. Depression. "Yes, me" stage. The realization comes that what they have been told is true, but it brings sadness and depression.

4. Resignation. "I don't want to die, but I'm tired of fighting." Bitterness is still present, and they have become sadly fatalistic.

5. Acceptance. "No one escapes death. It had to come sometime." The person now has inner and outer peace. As a woman dying of cancer wrote in her diary: "What can I do with the rest of my life? LIVE ALL OF IT!"

Many hospital chaplains would add a sixth stage: **Hope.** "I know that my Redeemer lives, and from my flesh I shall see God" (Job 19:25, 26). It is the work of the chaplain to move people as quickly as possible into Stages Five and Six. Dr. Kübler-Ross estimates that eighty percent of the patients in a nursing home for the aged are in a state of resignation, and perhaps that explains the sadness that so often seems present in such places. Those who reach Stage Five are truly blessed.

Photographer Mal Warshaw, who produced a book of pictures of dying persons, had this observation: "I noted that the faces of people who have a terminal disease, and who have come to terms with their impending death, have a look that is a marvelous combination of tranquillity and incredible power and insight." When one makes peace with death, there is nothing more that life can do to that person.

Dr. Kübler-Ross also observes in her books that persons intimately associated with a deceased person go through the same psychological process as the person facing death, particularly if that death is sudden. Their reaction to the death of a closely-loved one progressively is shock and denial, anger, depression, resignation and acceptance. It is well for people to realize that this process is natural and that their feelings and reactions are the same as those of the many others who have suffered the death of a loved one. Again it is the aim of the chaplain or counselor to move the survivor through this process as rapidly as possible. Survivors often have an unconscious guilt because they still survive. Often present, too, is a guilty feeling that they did not act better to the deceased or that they omitted things they should have done. Survivors also need to be taught to overcome death and its effects.

The Christian should avoid becoming too clinical or scientific about death, around which there will always be an aura of mystery. The believer in an afterlife has to seek out the moral and theological dimensions of death. In facing death, one needs to turn to his or her religious roots. In the Old Testament, long life was looked upon as God's favor while death was a punishment for sin. From the moment he ate from the tree, God promised, Adam was surely doomed to die (Gen 2:17, 3:3). In death one was cut off from God — in fact forgotten. "My couch is among the dead . . . whom you remember no longer and who are cut off from your care" (Ps 88:6). Baruch (2:17) saw the dead in the nether world as hopeless bodies from whom the spirit had been destroyed. It was not until late Judaism that the idea of resurrection, or the conquering of death, began to be proposed. The New Testament teaching of life in Christ was revolutionary.

In Christian theology, death is but a doorway to God and everlasting life. Death was transformed by Christ, who in becoming man took on all the consequences of being human, including death, the result of sin. By His death, Christ opened anew the gates of heaven and by His resurrection, He leads the people of God through suffering and death to eternal life. Thus Paul could quote Scripture: "Death, where is your victory? O death, where is your sting?" (1 Cor 15:15). The Christian dwells not in the shadow of death but in the light of eternal life.

The late Cardinal John Wright called death "the decisive moment" in every person's life. He did this, not because at the moment of death we have a decision to make, but because at that moment God's decision on our eternity will take place. Death marks the end of our probation or trial. At the moment of death each one of us has already decided whether he or she belongs to Christ or Adam. Once death comes, we no longer have choices. Each one of us receives our recompense, Paul tells us (2 Cor 5:10), "according to his life in the body."

Before death we are changeable creatures, but with death a transition takes place that is unchangeable. If a person dies in hatred to God, that hatred will continue throughout all eternity. If one dies in friendship with God, that direction is also immutable and will continue throughout eternity. There is an old spiritual axiom: "As you live, so shall you die." If we live with Christ, we will live with Him forever. If we reject Christ, we reject Him for all eternity. It is presumption and a mistake to expect a deathbed conversion. Death's first appearance in biblical history is the result of a man's sin. The conquering of death, proved by Christ's resurrection, was because of a man's obedience to the will of God.

A Christian death places us forever beyond the temptations of Satan and joins us forever to Christ in the Communion of Saints, and in this vast multitude we will accompany Jesus when at the end He returns all creation to the Father.

Since, therefore, death is such a decisive moment in the history of each individual, it is a foolish man or woman (Mt 25:1-13) who does not prepare for it. If we would die in union with Christ, we will live in union with Him. If we are to have this union, we must pray, because every prayer unites our will to God. "Pray always," Jesus told us. For many, prayer only comes into play when there is some need. Prayer is, however, far more than supplication. Prayer is primarily adoration, our praise of God and His greatness. I am reminded of an old Catholic woman in China, who could neither read nor write but who spent long hours in church. The missioner asked her what she did during all this time. "I just look at God," she replied, "and He looks at me."

Then there is prayer of reparation. Some saints have spent their whole lives seeking penances and trials to atone for the offenses of humanity against God. How seldom do we repair the damage done through sin! How rarely do we meditate on our own personal role in the Passion of Christ! Finally, there is the prayer of thanksgiving. God has given us not only life in this world but the opportunity of life forever in the world to come. He has surrounded us with the wonders of nature as a foretaste of what is to come. He has given us family, friends and the capacity to love them. Yet how seldom do we send our thanks heavenward.

Above all, Christ has given us the perfect means to prepare for death and eternal life — the sacraments! Each of the sacraments in its own way helps us to meet death.

Although we are reborn in baptism, freed from an inheritance of sin, baptism is really the gateway to heaven. Without baptism we cannot go beyond the gate. St. Paul tells us (Rom 6:4-5): "Through baptism into his death we were buried with him, so that, just as Christ was raised from the dead by the glory of the Father, we too might live a new life. If we have been united with Him through likeness to his death, so shall we be through a like resurrection."

While sin separates us from God, the Sacrament of Penance restores us to His life. The *Constitution on Indulgences* reminds us: "All men who walk this earth commit at least venial, so-called daily sins. All, therefore, need God's mercy to set them free from sin's penal consequences.'' Sin should make us aware of divine judgment, while the Sacrament of Penance reminds us of His love and our life in the Paschal mystery. And what greater reparation can we make to God than when, in the Sacrament of the Eucharist, we offer the Divine Victim to the Father and ourselves along with Him. If in the Eucharist we proclaim the death of the Lord, we likewise celebrate His resurrection and the promise of our own eternal life. Every communion should prepare us for union with Christ which is beyond death.

Marriage, which is a death to selfishness if it is to be successful, is also a mirror of the love that exists between Christ and His Church, the love which we will share in a very particular way after death. Confirmation is a renewal of our Christian Initiation. We are given a special strength of the Holy Spirit that will better enable us to meet death. The Sacrament of Anointing of the Sick is an immediate preparation for death. At the giving of Viaticum, the priest prays:

"Through the suffering, death and resurrection of Jesus Christ, may almighty God free you from all punishments in this life and in the life to come. May He open paradise to you and welcome you to the joy of eternal life.''

The priest is authorized by the power of the Holy See to bestow a plenary indulgence on the person in danger of death. This power comes from the keys given Peter: "Whatever you declare loosed on earth shall be loosed in heaven'' (Mt 16:19).

Those who lead their lives in union with Jesus Christ and His Church need have no fear of death. They can approach the hour of death with confidence that "They will see the Lord face to face, and His name will be written on their foreheads. It will never be night again and they will not need lamplight or sunlight, because the Lord God will be shining on them. They will reign for ever and ever'' (Rev 22:4-5).

CHAPTER 7

Heaven

IT WAS ONE OF THE UNINTENDED RESULTS
of the Second Vatican Council that preoccupation with
the afterlife should lessen. Although the Bible tells us
that "Here we have no lasting city, but we seek the
city which is to come" (Heb 13:14, RSV), nevertheless
many have become more concerned with the City of
Man than the City of God. There is a relevancy to the
here and now which could give the impression that
there is an irrelevancy to the world to come. There is a
suggestion that some television reruns are more en-
joyable than the beatific vision. *The Pastoral Constitution on the Church in the Modern World* was
interpreted by activists as their marching orders to
become part of that world, overlooking the essential
fact that while the Church must exist in the world, it
cannot be part of the world (Jn 17:16). Yet for many,
regard for the needy neighbor, service to the poor, and
the corporal works of mercy have become the ultimate
goal of religion.

John Shea in his *What a Modern Catholic Believes about Heaven and Hell* writes: "Christians
everywhere are burning the castles of heaven and

quenching the fires of hell. In the post-Vatican II church the word is out. Religion does not mean other-worldly preoccupation but this-worldly service. . . . The modern Catholic who values pleasure and celebrates life often associates heaven and hell with their negation.''

Nevertheless, if one reads the *Pastoral Constitution* without being very selective, as is so often the case, one finds eschatological overtones. While the Christian must be concerned with the good of his or her neighbor, the ultimate end of the Church is not in Peace and Justice Commissions but in the realization of the Paschal mystery. The aim of the *Constitution* is not the creation of Utopia on earth, an impossibility, but the salvation of the individual and the community. The Church does have a concern with the present society and its conditions, but its real end is the world that will be brought to fulfillment in the resurrection. The last day is the important day, not today. Our present concern with injustice is so that all ''will awaken to a lively hope (the gift of the Holy Spirit) that they will one day be admitted to the haven of surpassing peace and happiness in their homeland radiant with the glory of the Lord.''

So, while there are those who would be indifferent or pass off heaven as not of importance at the moment, there are others who are contemptuous of it. ''Heaven for climate, hell for company,'' wittingly remarks a J.M. Barrie character. ''Work and pray, live on hay,'' sang the old Wobblies, ''You'll get pie in the sky when you die — it's a lie!'' Thoreau was more right than cynical when he observed: ''Heaven might be defined as the place that men avoid.'' Machiavelli, who at least admitted the existence of afterworlds, said on his deathbed, "I desire to go to Hell, not to Heaven. In Hell I shall enjoy the company of popes, kings and princes, but in Heaven are only beggars, monks, hermits and apostles."

Such remarks show a lack of appreciation for and ignorance of heaven. That even good Christians misunderstand and misinterpret heaven should not be surprising. As Father Vincent P. McCorry wrote, "The Oriental concept which makes the realms of bliss a place where man may have three hundred and fifty excellent meals a day and as many wives as he wants would appear to be preferable to the celestial picture which exists in many Christian minds."

Perhaps the problem arises in trying to describe a place from which no one has ever returned to tell us what it is like; in trying to imagine something beyond imagination. St. Paul, who was seldom at a loss for words, had to fall back on Isaiah and admit (1 Cor 2:9): "Eye has not seen, ear has not heard, nor has it so much as dawned on man what God has prepared for those who love him." Which might be paraphrased in modern idiom, "I don't know what heaven will be like, but I know it will be supergood." St. Thomas Aquinas could argue about aureoles and crowns, and who in heaven would wear what size, and while the modern has little care about crowns, he or she can understand happiness, and that is the bottom line of heaven. Maybe we have tried to be too descriptive of what we cannot describe and confused people, like the little girl who told her father: "I don't want to go to heaven because I don't want wings." In trying to re-create paradise, we may be trying to say too much. Thomas Fuller notes that heaven is a cheap purchase no matter what it costs. We might be better off selling the sizzle than an imprecise theology.

The yearning for a paradise lost is ingrained in the traditions of mankind. The historian and philosopher Will Durant has written: "The legend of Paradise appears in almost all folklore — in Egypt, Tibet, Babylonia, Persia, Greece, Polynesia, Mexico, and others. Most of these Edens had forbidden trees, and were supplied with serpents or dragons that stole immortality from men, or otherwise poisoned Paradise." The scriptural modernist uses this fact to condemn the Book of Genesis as purloined legends. However, the fact that the legend of paradise appears in such diverse folklore suggests that it must have had a common origin lost in the mists of time before the great migrations, and that this history of early man must have arisen in some catacylsmic event. The consolation of religion is the knowledge that paradise lost can be paradise regained.

The whole thrust of the New Testament is to the kingdom of God. "Every heart to heaven aspires," wrote the poet. But the desire for heaven is more than mere hope.The late Jacques Maritain saw history as a movement toward the kingdom of God. He warned that it will not be part of history but only come at the end of history. The nature of this kingdom has long engaged the speculation of theologians. Because we tend to think in concrete terms, heaven often takes on physical forms, and our interpretation is colored by anthropomorphisms. The Father is pictured as an old man with a white beard sitting on an ornate throne. A great deal of this imagery came from the Bible itself, whose writers were trying to describe the indescribable. Spirit cannot be drawn, and God's image cannot be confined within the lines of an illustration. In the Old Testament God was represented as living in that vast space above the superior waters which hung above the firmament which contained the sun, moon and stars. The waters were kept from falling on the earth by a great wall whose floodgates were opened by God from time to time to allow rain and snow to fall upon earth. Earth was man's domain and heaven was reserved as the abode of God. For man to aspire to heaven was as prideful as the attempt to build the tower of Babel. Isaiah (14:13-15) tells of the vanity of such ambition and its punishment. The ancient Jews pictured God sitting on a throne, contained in a palace, and surrounded by His heavenly court. This primitive image still has life today.

In the Israelite conception, although God was at a far distance, He was not remote. The Old Testament continually attests to His presence among His people on earth. His concern with the affairs of humanity was not that of an inaccessible supervisor but of a participant. He spoke with Adam and Eve, punished Cain, instructed Noah, and chatted with Abram (Abraham), sometimes in person (Gen 17:1) and sometimes in a vision (Gen 15:1). Moreover, God also sent His angels to be among men. Angels first appear after the Fall to prevent Adam from reentering paradise (Gen 3:24). Abraham entertained angels (Gen 18); Lot was warned by them (Gen 19); Jacob in a vision saw angels going up and down from heaven, and he called the place where this happened (Bethel) "the abode of God" (Gen 28). The Archangel Raphael became the friend, guide and protector of young Tobias (or Tobiah).

From the Book of Deuteronomy on, the theology of

Israel begins to change. God still communicates with His people but remains in heaven. In Exodus God spoke to His people from elevated heights. Moses had to climb Mount Sinai (Ex 19:3) to converse with God. Somehow His presence was there, and Moses alone could go close to it (Ex 24:1-2), and when He did make an appearance it was in the form of a burning bush, which was more a sign of the presence of God than of His actual Being. Throughout the remaining books of the Old Testament, the God of heaven who knows all things is the dominant force in the history of Israel, and the hope arises that somehow the just might be joined to God in heaven. The Psalmist (73:24) prays to God that "in the end you will receive me in glory." Although Isaiah's prayer was for the restoration of Zion, his true hope was eternal life with the Lord. Elijah, going up to heaven in a fiery chariot, was a prototype of what was to come. Salvation was for humankind somehow to be joined to God.

Isaiah's prayer, that God "would rend the heavens and come down" (63:19), came to fulfillment with the birth of Jesus Christ, and the whole thrust of the New Testament is man's intimacy with God through His Son. If humanity could not rise to heaven of its own accord, it could through Christ. He was the gate of heaven. "No one," Jesus told Thomas, "comes to the Father but through me" (Jn 14:6), and then He solved the great problem of history about seeing and knowing the Father by reminding Philip, "Whoever has seen me has seen the Father" (Jn 14:9). Jesus rested His claims in His own resurrection and proved them by rising on the third day. He goes to heaven (Jn 14:3) "to prepare a place for you, and then I shall come back and take you with me, that where I am you also may be." Thus heaven became the end and fulfillment of salvation history, and God is "all in all" (1 Cor 15:28). The *New Catholic Encyclopedia* states: "Heaven is the state of happiness of those who have died in Christ. Although it is also a place, this is of secondary importance." Despite this assertion, the Church has never defined heaven as an area requiring space. Pius XII in defining in 1950 the dogma of the Assumption never mentioned Mary going to a place but only referred to the Virgin being "taken up in glory." Most theologians of the past have referred to heaven as a place, largely because Jesus and His Mother are there both in body and soul, and a body requires space. But the resurrected body is not the same as the earthly body. It is what theologians term a glorified body, about whose exact nature we are not sure. The glorified body of Jesus could pass through walls and closed doors (Jn 20:19) and hence did not seem to require space, yet St. Thomas Aquinas in his *Summa* continually refers to the place occupied by a glorified body. So theologians disagree, and the Church, as such, has taken no defined position. John, in his First Epistle, best sums up the situation: "We are God's children now; what we shall later be has not yet come to light" (1 Jn 3:2).

Heaven has been variously described. It is called a place of total happiness where there will be no pain or suffering, where we will be filled with all we need. The supreme happiness, theologians tells us, is in the beatific vision, which they define as the true end of mankind. Karl Rahner calls it "God himself as self-communicating goodness." The beatific vision, according to Rahner, is "the full and definitive experience of the direct self-communication of God himself to the individual human being." St. Paul puts it more simply: it is seeing God "face to face" (1 Cor 13:12). John (1 Jn 3:2) says almost the same thing: "We shall be like him for we shall see him as he is."

Intuitive knowledge of God is the end for which we are destined. This is not something we can arrive at ourselves by our own powers but is the free gift of God as a reward for remaining faithful to Him during this period of trial on earth. This desire for God is implanted in every human heart, although it may not always be recognized. Augustine says, "You have made us for Yourself, O Lord, and our hearts are restless until they find rest in you." The English poet, Francis Thompson, in his poem *The Hound of Heaven* (Morehouse), describes man's quest for happiness, seeking it in all types of pleasures, only at the end to hear God say, 'I am He Whom thou seekest!'"

Philosophers tell us that the object of the will is doing good; that is, whatever we choose to do, we so choose because we think we are choosing good. Even the thief robbing a bank does so because he believes he is choosing what is good for himself. Even the suicide believes that his or her act at the moment is good. The theologian goes a step beyond the philosopher and tells us that the true object of the will is God, the Supreme Good. God has placed within each human heart an instinct for Himself. Worldly cares and concerns can make this voice of God within us hard to hear, but it is there. This often-unrecognized desire is a yearning for the beatific vision. Yet this supernatural desire is not something we can obtain by natural powers alone. While it makes us aware that we want God, it does not make us aware of what God is. While our destiny is supernatural union with God, our understanding of Him is His own free gift. Once given, it is a gift never lost. A question that often arises in any discussion of heaven is our relationship with those we love on earth. Will we see them? Will we know them? Will we have any relationship with them? The answer is yes. It is found in the Church's doctrine of the communion of saints. We will always be the children of our parents and the parents of our children. God does not wipe out the past but joins it to future happiness. Our love for others is a spiritual quality which endures. Those to whom we are related on earth will find us related to them in heaven. Although God will make all things new to us, He will not destroy what is good in the old. In heaven we will have everything that is needed to make us happy, and what mother could be happy without the presence of those she loves?

In heaven we will also enjoy the company of the elect, or blessed — all those who have also achieved salvation. In a land that is truly our home we shall know and share eternal life with all our brothers and sisters in Christ. We will be in the company of the Blessed Virgin and the saints. We will comprehend the nature of and enjoy the fruits of the Mystical Body. We will be one in accord with all the court of heaven. Our contacts will not be the same as human contacts were on earth because we will be different beings whose former world has passed away. Yet so overcoming was a vision of the joys of heaven given to the author of the Book of Revelation that he could only respond at the end with a great cry: "Amen! Come, Lord Jesus!"

Will there be total equality in heaven? Not really. We will all enjoy the essential knowledge of God but in varying degrees according to our capabilities and merits. Jesus said that in heaven there are many dwelling places (Jn 14:2) and that the Son of Man will repay each according to his or her conduct (Mt 16:27). St. Paul puts it this way: "Even among the stars, one differs from another in brightness. So it is with the resurrection of the dead" (1 Cor 15:41-42). St. Francis de Sales amplifies St. Paul by writing, "As star differs from star in brightness, so men will be different from one another in glory, in proportion as they have been different in graces and merits." The martyrs and the saints who served God so well on earth will be more exalted than those who only made heaven by the grace of an extra prayer. Will this difference give rise to envy? No, because envy has no place in heaven. A one-gallon pail is just as full as a five-gallon pail; when each is filled to the brim, neither can contain more. Each in heaven has all the happiness that he or she is capable of receiving.

Each of us must not be too concerned with the nature of heaven because as the Bible tells us our earthly minds simply cannot grasp what is in store for us. Moreover, the devil can use vain speculation about heaven to turn us away from God. Thomas Merton reminds us of this when he writes in *The Seven Storey Mountain* (Doubleday): "The devil is no fool. He can get people feeling about heaven the way they ought to feel about hell. He can make them fear the means of grace the way they do not fear sin."

What each must understand is that earth is only a place of pilgrimage and that heaven is our native land, destined by God to those who serve Him. We have no lasting cities on earth, but we do have a home that will endure for all eternity awaiting us at the end of this life. So we live now in hope and expectation, awaiting at the end of our days that invitation of Jesus: "Come, you have my Father's blessing! Inherit the kingdom prepared for you from the creation of the world" (Mt 25:34).

CHAPTER 8

Hell

THE CONTEMPORARY CHRISTIAN
would rather not think about hell; at least that is the
impression that many of them give.

John Shea, in *What a Modern Catholic Believes
about Heaven and Hell*, writes: "Today the flames
of hell burn low. The devil who once lurked in book-
stores, in the bushes at the park, and at office parties
is nowhere to be found. Catholics who once mapped the
terrain of the afterlife and did not hesitate to speculate
about who was going where are now more timid. Hell
as a conscious part of the Catholic make-up is definite-
ly on the decline. . . . Whether there has actually ever
been damnation or not is beyond human knowledge. No
one can draw limits to God's love or make a final, pes-
simistic remark about the use of human freedom. The
concept of hell as 'eternal torment' is the cultural picture of another time and another place."

The typical purveyor of modernist teaching leaves
open the possibility of hell while affirming its lack of
probability. These modern theorists and their watered-
down theories are undermining belief in eternal
punishment. The problem of reconciling the mercy of

God with the justice of God is one that has troubled men of conscience for long centuries — from the earliest days of the Church, in fact. It is understandable that out of compassion and love for others one would hope that no one went to hell. "The God, whose love is infinity, must be still less willing to see men in such straits," Dom Bede Jarrett wrote not too many years ago.

Long centuries before that, however, St. Augustine considered the same problem and concluded, "The perpetual death of the damned, that is, their separation from the life of God will go on without end and will be their common lot, regardless of what people prompted by human sentiments may conjure up about different kinds of punishment or a mitigation or interruption of torments." Indeed, Ezekiel (33:11) records, "As I live, says the Lord, I have no pleasure in the death of the wicked man, rather let him turn from his evil way and live." And there is the nub of the question. God does not desire any one to go to hell, but it is the person himself who seeks hell by his actions and deliberate separation from God.

Dante's sign over the gateway of hell — "Abandon hope, you who enter here" — may be a sad one but it is there nevertheless.

The word "hell" is of Teutonic origin, and the name is given to the place in German mythology which was the abode of the dead. Originally it did not mean a place of suffering or damnation but merely the abode of the dead. In Hebrew the word was *sheol* and in Greek *hades*. This was the "hell" to which Christ went after His resurrection to lead the souls of the saved to heaven. The Hebrews had a place of fiery punishment called *gehenna* (Greek: *tartarus*); this is what we can call hell. Jesus used the view of a separated sheol prevailing in His time in His parable of Poor Lazarus. Both the rich man and the beggar die and go to sheol, but Lazarus is in the bosom of Abraham while the rich man is tortured in flames. The rich man begs Lazarus to bring him a few drops of water to ease his suffering, but Abraham tells him that cannot be because between them and the rich man there is a great abyss which cannot be crossed.

The notion of hell is not solely a Christian or Jewish idea. It existed in various cultures, deriving from the common opinion that if good was to be rewarded, evil had to be punished. "The descent to hell is easy," the Latin poet Virgil wrote in the *Aeneid*, "the gates stand open night and day." An Indian manuscript, *Mahabharata*, dating from about 800 B.C., records: "A terrible hell awaits the wicked, a profound abyss of utter misery, into the depths of which bad men fall headlong and mourn their doom for countless years." The fact that it is the sinner that makes his hell rather than God was considered in another Indian writing, *Dhammapada*, dating about five centuries before Christ: "It is the iron's own rust that destroys it. It is the sinner's own acts that bring him to hell."

Over the years men have given their own interpretation to hell. Niccolò Machiavelli expressed on his deathbed the desire to go to hell because the company was better. The cynical George Bernard Shaw called hell "a perpetual holiday." The misanthropic Jean-Paul Sartre morosely opined, "Hell is other people." Thomas Merton, in *Seeds of Contemplation* (New Directions), also saw people as a problem but in a more Christian way: "Hell is where no one has anything in common with anybody else except the fact that they all hate one another and cannot get away from one another and from themselves." The *Enchiridion* sums up Catholic dogma on hell in this manner: Those who die in original sin or grave personal sin immediately descend into hell, where they are punished by different punishments, namely, by loss or lack of vision of God for sin both original and personal, and by the sensation or torments by which those who lived evilly are punished for all eternity. At the consummation of the world there will be a resurrection even of the damned with their own bodies. There will follow a universal judgment through Christ, who renders to each according to his or her works, and when this is done there will never be any metamorphosis of the demons or impious men.

Catholic teaching on hell is rooted in the teaching of Christ. Jesus spoke often about hell, and to deny the existence of hell, or to affirm that God's mercy would not send anyone there, is to negate what Christ repeatedly said. There are more than two dozen references to hell in the New Testament. The authoritative Athanasian Creed, which was not composed by St. Athanasius despite its name, declares, "At his (Christ's) coming all men will have to rise again with their bodies and will render an account of their own deeds: and those who have done good, will go into life everlasting, but those who have done evil, into eternal fire. . . . This is the Catholic faith; unless everyone believes this faithfully and firmly, he cannot be saved." The last sentence refers to the entire Creed as well as the sentence quoted. Repeated statements by popes and councils confirm this ancient teaching.

Karl Rahner writes: "In its official teaching the Church has defined the existence of hell and its eternity against the doctrine of the apocatastasis put forward by Origen and other ancient writers. Asserting implicitly an important principle of hermeneutics, the Church eliminated temporal patterns from the existence of the dead, by affirming against the doctrine of an intermediate state of the lost before the general judgment that entry into hell takes place immediately after death. A certain distinction is made between the loss of the vision of God (*poena damni*) and the pain of sense (*poena sensus*), but apart from this there is no official declaration on the nature of the pains of hell, though the difference of punishments in hell is mentioned.''

(*The New Catholic Encyclopedia* simplifies the word apocatastasis as that Greek name derived from Acts 3:21, given to the doctrine of the ultimate salvation of all rational creatures.)

Thus, while the Church tells us that hell exists and people are punished there for eternity in different ways and to different degrees, beyond that we really know nothing. Another modern theologian of repute, Joseph Ratzinger, has written: ''The theological exposition of the dogma cannot be primarily devoted to an objectivating speculation on the other world. It must apply itself above all to bringing out the real relevance of the affirmation of hell to human existence. Hence it cannot be the task of theology to go into details about supposed facts of the next life, such as the number of the damned, the severity of their pain, and so on. But it has the task of maintaining the dogma of hell in all its realistic claim. For without this claim it cannot fulfill its task as part of revelation, which is to bring men to control their lives in the light of the real possibility of eternal failure and to recognize revelation as a claim of utmost seriousness. This salutary purpose of the dogma must always set bounds to and provide the guiding lines for all speculation in this matter."

In speaking of the punishment of hell, Rahner makes an important distinction which some modernist theologians ought to keep in mind. When we think of punishment, we ordinarily think of it in vindictive terms, for example: the state punishes the criminal with incarceration for having broken the law. Rahner affirms that this image is not suitable when explaining the doctrine of hell. He says, "The just God is 'active' in the punishment of hell only insofar as he does not release man from the reality of the definitive state which man himself has achieved on his own behalf, contradictory though this state be to the world as God's creation."

It is not God who sentences the sinner to hell but the sinner himself by his free choices. The composer Gian-Carlo Menotti had this in mind when he wrote in the *Saturday Review*: "For me, the conception of hell lies in two words: 'too late.' " God enables us to reform our lives at any time up to the moment of death, but once that moment comes it is too late to do anything else. As we die, we remain. If we have chosen to live cut off from the grace of God, that is the way we die and remain. To blame God for this choice is ridiculous. Thus to those who say that God can send no one to hell — the answer is that this is correct. God does not send us to hell, we send ourselves.

God has given us free will that we might choose to believe in Him. Hell results not so much from sin but from this unbelief (Jn 16:9). The Father sent the Son and sends the Spirit in His saving work. The Son revealed Himself to us and showed us the way to the Father. The Spirit continually prompts us to seek the Father, and it is in the ultimate rejection of the Spirit that we find the true unforgivable sin, a term the old catechisms called "the sin against the Holy Ghost."

So much for the developing theological concepts of hell. The dogmatic teaching of the Church is clear and firm, going back to the New Testament and apostolic teaching. The earliest credal formulas all portray Christ as the judge of the living and the dead, presuming the judgment to be between heaven and hell. The Church has made two definitions regarding hell to which Catholics must give assent. The first is that the punishment of hell is unending (eternal). This was defined by Pope Vigilius in the canons against Origen: "If anyone says or holds that the punishment of the demons and of impious men is temporary and that it will have an end at some time, that is to say, there will be a complete restoration of the demons or impious men, let him be anathema." The second is that punishment takes place immediately after death. This was proclaimed "on apostolic authority which will prevail forever" by Benedict XII in the 1336 edict *Benedictus Deus*, which said: "We declare that according to the common arrangement of God, the souls of those who depart in actual mortal sin immediately after their death descend to hell where they are tortured by infernal punishments."

Neither of these declarations was made in a vacuum but was a reaction to teachings of their time. Origen, much moved by Christ's saving love, admitted that sin brought separation from God, but he believed that the punishments for these sins were corrective and would end when the new world was created at the end of time. Another opinion that lasted for a long time was that of Justin who taught that punishment of the damned would be delayed until after the general judgment. That some of Origen's arguments and other condemned theories arise again even today shows that theologians continue to wrestle with the nature and meaning of hell. Always, however, we must be careful that balanced judgment is not ruled by sentiment. It is one thing to hope that every human will be saved and another to assert the hope as fact. It is one thing to trust in Christ's love and saving sacrifice, and another to deny that people can reject it.

Are there many people in hell? We simply do not know. The Church has defined nothing beyond the two articles mentioned above. However, if we take Scripture at face value, it would seem that condemnation to hell is not a rarity — for example, at the last judgment when the Son of Man separates the sheep and goats (Mt 25:31-46) and says to the goats, "Out of my sight, you condemned, into that everlasting fire prepared for the devils and his angels." While no numbers or percentages are given, the implication is given that the army of the condemned is not inconsequential. In His parable on the wedding banquet, Christ concluded (Mt 22:14): "The invited are many, the elect are few." As part of His Sermon on the Mount, Jesus indicated the selectivity of heaven: "Enter through the narrow gate. The gate that leads to damnation is wide, the road is clear, and many choose to travel it. But how narrow is the gate that leads to life, how rough the road, and how few there are who find it!" (Mt 7:13-14).

There are other texts, but the aforementioned give the picture that Scripture paints. If one is to take them at face value, it would appear that far more are going to be lost than saved. This thought even troubled the disciples. Once after Jesus had finished commenting on the difficulty the rich would have to enter heaven, Matthew tells us they were overwhelmed (Mt 19:25) and exclaimed, "Then who can be saved?" Jesus told them, "For man it is impossible; but for God all things are possible." The paradox that Jesus is creating here is that a person can be saved despite his riches but only by corresponding with God's grace, that mysterious element of salvation which in its totality is beyond human comprehension. It is that same grace that leads to deathbed conversions, which are often a scandal to those who do not understand its workings. In the end we must leave numbers to the providence of God but be concerned with our own salvation.

Another question theological pundits have debated over the centuries is whether or not the fires of hell are real fires as we know them on earth or are used to symbolize intense suffering, particularly the burning yearning for what has been lost. Ancient Jewish cosmology placed sheol deep in the bowels of the earth, and since volcanoes erupted from time to time, with fiery lava coming from deep within the earth, the notion of a fiery hell came into being. The New Testament speaks of fire in relation to hell more than thirty times, referring to it also as everlasting and unquenchable.

There are few theologians today who would affirm that the fire of hell is true fire. As Father John Hardon, S.J., observes in *The Catholic Catechism*, "Dante is not the Church." It might be more accurate to speak of the eternal punishment of hell than to think of physical flames. As early as the third century, St. Cyprian was following this practice when he wrote: "The pain of punishment then will be without the fruit of penitence; weeping will be useless and prayer ineffectual. Too late they will believe in eternal punishment who would not believe in eternal life." In the end it makes little difference if the torments of hell are real fire or like real fire. There is little consolation in the distinction for the condemned soul. Suffering in the soul can be far more exquisite than bodily pain. It would be no consolation to tell a soul in hell, "But it isn't real fire!" The tortures of suffering are real, no matter the cause.

Medieval theologians argued about the location of hell. St. Thomas Aquinas settled the question for himself: "I do not believe that man can know the position of hell." Another debate of the past is the nature of punishment inflicted on various sinners. Pope St. Gregory considered this question in the sixth century when he asked, "Is there one fire in hell, or, according to the diversity of sinners, are there as many kinds of fire prepared in that place? The fire in hell is one, but it does not torment all sinners in the same way. Everyone there, according to the quantity of his sin, has the measure of his pain."

The Teaching of Christ notes, "The punishment of hell is great but it is in no way excessive. Faith teaches that God is just and merciful, that no one is punished more harshly than he deserves." The same arguments given previously about the difference of rewards in heaven apply to the difference of punishments in hell. In short, hell is occupied by people who refuse to choose God, and their punishment, both qualitatively and quantitatively, is of their own making. The Psalmist (9:17) said it succinctly a long time ago: "In passing sentence, the Lord is manifest; the wicked are trapped by the work of their own hands."

CHAPTER 9

Purgatory

IT IS AN UNFORTUNATE FACT
of religious history that purgatory was an emotional
red flag for many reformers who were so incensed
about the abuse of indulgences that they threw out the
baby along with the bath water. While Martin Luther
admitted purgatory, he did at one point compare it to
"an uncertainty." Calvin at the other extreme saw it
as a "dreadful blasphemy against Christ." Even today
the Catholic doctrine of purgatory seems unreasonably
to upset fundamentalists and pentecostal Christians.

The Church's teaching on purgatory is quite simple:
that there exists after death a place, state or condition
where those who die in union with God but who are not
free of all imperfection, and who have not properly
atoned for unforgiven venial sins or for the temporal
punishment due forgiven sins, are purified before they
enter heaven. Jesus in the Beatitudes blessed the pure
in heart, promising that they would see God, but to be
pure in heart means to be free of fault and unattached
to any kind of sin, even sin of a lesser nature which
does not bring eternal death. The only people who
leave this world in this manner are the saints, who

pass directly into the presence of God. Those who die in mortal sin, namely by free choice separating themselves from God, pass directly into eternal punishment. But what happens to that great body of people who did not die as saints, still having faults and imperfections? What happens to atonement necessary for sins forgiven by God? According to the Church, these people go to a temporary place of purification called purgatory.

Although purgatory is not specifically mentioned by name in Scripture, its existence is closely related to divine justice. The whole thrust of Scripture is for the mercy of God to be shown to His people. Proverbs (20:9) asks: "Who can say, 'I have made my heart clean, I am cleansed from my sin'?" Again the Psalmist asks, "Who can ascend the mountain of the Lord?" and gives his own reply, "He whose hands are sinless, whose heart is clean" (Ps 24:3-4). How many people could honestly say that was a picture of themselves? Yet if God is just and renders each according to his or her due, some atonement is needed for imperfections. The place for this purification is purgatory, not hell.

It is a fact that revelation in the Bible was an ongoing and developing process. God did not reveal His entire plan for man to Adam or to Abraham or to Moses. Each built on what went before. So too did biblical theology develop. We noted in a previous chapter how the biblical notion of sheol and hell developed. Thus when Sirach (7:33) advises his readers "Withhold not your kindness from the dead," he was probably speaking of more than obsequies but with the resurrection in mind, a teaching then coming into prominence. In the two centuries before Christ, prayer and sacrifice for the dead became of concern, a care that is only reasonable in consideration of an afterlife with God.

The teaching of purgatory finds its clearest Old Testament reference in the Second Book of Maccabees (a book which the reformers discarded from the Protestant Bible, being greatly influenced by that very fact). In 2 Maccabees 12:38-46, it is told how Judas Maccabeus took up a collection among his soldiers to send to Jerusalem for expiatory prayers for their dead companions because he had the resurrection of the dead in mind, adding, "Thus he made atonement for the dead that they might be freed from this sin." This perfectly describes purgatory, the place where we are freed from the effects of sin, where the prayers of the living can help us. Some modern exegetes would probably differ in this interpretation, but it is the traditional interpretation of the Church, and to get another meaning means to do violence to the patent meaning of the text.

While the New Testament does not specifically name purgatory, Jesus spoke of sins that would be forgiven in the world to come (Mt 12:32). Although Jesus tended to speak in contrasts, in black and whites, in sheep and goats, nowhere does He suggest that salvation will come only to those who have achieved perfection in this life, yet that would be what was implied if there was no purgatory. Although the doctrine of purgatory becomes logical from the teaching of the New Testament, the Scriptures themselves should not be stretched into proving what is not explicitly said.

It is tradition that the Catholic Church uses in defending its teaching. The Catholic Church accepts literally and actively Christ's promise that the Holy Spirit would guide His Church "to all truth" (Jn 16:13). In fact, one of the reasons Jesus gives for His death is that the Holy Spirit will be enabled to come into the Church (Jn 16:7). Thus the teaching of the Apostles and their successors, the Fathers of the Church, carry a weight equal to Scripture. Catholics call this teaching Sacred Tradition. The Second Vatican Council, in its *Dogmatic Constitution on Divine Revelation*, spoke of the great importance of the Gospels in Catholic teaching because of the presence of the Holy Spirit in their writing. The council, however, also points out that God's concern for His Church did not end with the Gospels or the Apostles but continues through their successors.

"In order to keep the Gospel forever whole and alive within the Church," says the council, "the apostles left bishops as their successors, 'handing over their own teaching role' to them. This sacred Tradition, therefore, and sacred Scripture of both the Old and New Testament are like a mirror in which the pilgrim Church on earth looks at God . . . . Therefore the apostles, handing on what they themselves had received, warn the faithful to hold fast to the traditions which they have learned. . . . Now what was handed on by the apostles includes everything which contributes to the holiness of life and the increase in faith of the People of God; and so the Church, in her teaching, life and worship, perpetuates and hands on to all generations all that she herself is, all that she believes" (Nos. 7 and 8).

This digression was made to show the importance of tradition in the Catholic Church, and it is that same tradition which establishes purgatory.

It was a general belief in the early Church that souls after death, except for martyrs, went to a place of purification and atonement for sins committed during life. Tertullian wrote that the "last farthing" of the Gospel (Mt 5:26, now translated "last penny") meant the smallest offenses "which had to be compensated before the Resurrection," adding that no one should therefore deny the belief that some compensatory discipline had to be applied. Since this atonement could not be done in heaven, it had to be done in a place which came to be called purgatory.

St. Gregory of Nyssa wrote, "A man will not be able to participate in divinity until the cleansing fire will have purged him of every fault which has found its way into his soul." St. Gregory the Great also declared, "I know that at the end of this life some will do penance by purgatorial flames." St. Augustine testified, "What is not remitted in this world is remitted in the world to come." Origen, Cyprian, Ephrem, Ambrose, John Chrysostom and many others testify to the early belief in purgatory, and so do writers over the centuries until our own time when such as Karl Adam saw purgatory as a "thoroughfare to the Father." Thus purgatory is not a medieval invention, but its existence has been affirmed from the earliest days of the Church.

In answer to the Protestant reformers who denied their Church's teaching on purgatory, the Council of Trent (1545-1563) decreed: "Whereas the Catholic Church, instructed by the Holy Spirit, has from the sacred writings and ancient tradition of the Fathers taught in sacred councils and very recently in this ecumenical synod that there is a purgatory, and that souls detained there are helped by the suffrages of the faithful, but principally by the acceptable sacrifice of the altar; the holy synod enjoins on bishops that they diligently endeavor that the sound doctrine concerning purgatory, transmitted by the holy Fathers and sacred councils, be believed, maintained, taught, and everywhere proclaimed by the faithful of Christ." This basic teaching had also been affirmed for Catholics by the Councils of Florence (1438-1445) and Lyons (1245).

Theological teaching on the nature of purgatory is largely speculative. We have no idea how long a soul remains in purgatory, since there is no time in the next world that is measured in hours or days or years. The suffering of purgatory could be intense and short, or it could be prolonged. There is no body of opinion on this question.

Purgatory might be best described as a bittersweet experience. The soul is agonized by the separation from God, and yet there is the confident hope that this union with divinity will truly take place. St. Catherine of Genoa, in her treatise on purgatory, concurs in this opinion: "The soul in purgatory feels great happiness and great sorrow, the one does not hinder the other." Many theologians hold that this sense of loss is the real punishment of purgatory. The soul realizes that it is cut off from reaching God by venial sins and failings that could have been easily avoided, and which could have been atoned for in life. The realization that by its own doing it is separated from beatific sight of the Creator causes the pain of loss which is the agony of purgatory. St. Bonaventure, Suarez and St. Catherine of Genoa were of this opinion. Suarez however made the distinction that the degree of sanctity of the soul could make this loss less intense.

Other theologians stress the pain of sense. St. Augustine was of this opinion: "This fire of purgatory will be more severe than any pain that can be felt, seen or conceived in this world." St. Thomas Aquinas agreed with him: "It follows that the pain of purgatory, both of loss and sense, surpasses all the pains of this life." Both Augustine and Aquinas believed that the pain of sense was caused by real fire; however, this is not a required belief. The Eastern Church long before rejected the idea of real fire. Whether or not one accepts the notion of true fire, the general theological opinion is that there is some sort of positive suffering in purgatory. In the past there have been some repulsive and terrifying writings on purgatory based on supposed private revelations. The Council of Trent advises preachers to avoid preaching which is based on idle curiosity and superstition, and on those things which do not edify listeners. This advice is given in its Decree Concerning Purgatory and was in answer to some of the graphic preaching of the day.

Some theologians of older times held that the guilt of sin was removed upon the entrance to purgatory because the soul realized its yearning for God and made an intense act of love. However, this is not the current opinion, nor is it reflected in the revised funeral liturgy which repeatedly prays, "Forgive whatever wrong he (she) may have done during his (her) life on earth." Those who write on purgatory today seem to agree on a threefold purpose: (1) the removal of guilt of venial sin; (2) removal of inclination toward sin, and (3) removal of temporal punishment due to sin. Some have difficulty with the second, but the best opinion is that one's nature does not suddenly change at death and inclinations held at the moment of passing carry over and must be purged. Sin is not merely an external act but it affects the whole personality and is more deeply rooted in the psyche than the person realizes. One of the purposes of purgatory is to make a new person who will share the new creation that is to come. This view gives a positive aspect to purgatory rather than the negative old view of purgatory as a place of punishment. The certitude of salvation makes all of this not only acceptable but desired.

The Council of Trent in its Profession of Faith stated what Catholics must believe about purgatory: "I steadfastly hold that a purgatory exists, and that souls detained there are aided by the prayers of the faithful." The statement contains the two points that are required for faith. As regards the second, the Church allows indulgences to be applied to souls in purgatory, of which more will be said in Chapter 10. The foundation for the second point is in the Church's doctrine of Communion of Saints, the intersharing of all the People of God — on earth, in heavenly glory and in purgatory — with Christ, and in each other by faith, grace, prayer and good works. This means that any action of any member affects all the others. Thus the souls in purgatory can be aided by prayer, penances and indulgences. The degree of this assistance, of course, depends upon the will of God, but Jesus promised that what was asked in His name (Jn 14:14) would be done. God answers our prayers, sometimes in His own way and for His own reasons, and He is particularly attentive to those who are most dear to Him.

The most recent affirmation of the Church in the doctrine of purgatory was given by the Second Vatican Council in its *Dogmatic Constitution on the Church* (51) when the bishops of the world declared: "This sacred council accepts loyally the venerable faith of our ancestors in the living communion which exists between us and our brothers who are in the glory of heaven or who have not yet been purified after their death;

and it proposes again the decrees of the Second Council of Nicea, of the Council of Florence, and of the Council of Trent. At the same time, in keeping with its pastoral preoccupations, this council urges all concerned to remove or correct any abuses, excesses or defects, which may have crept in here or there, and so to restore all things that Christ and God may be more fully praised.''

Thus the ancient tradition of the Church is reaffirmed for moderns as a reminder that although we live in the here and now, there is a world to come — a world where each will be rendered his or her due.

CHAPTER 10

Indulgences

IT IS CLEAR TODAY THAT MARTIN LUTHER
was correct in his condemnation of John Tetzel and his
preaching of indulgences. The Dominican friar had
come into the Germanic regions with the authority of a
papal bull issued by Pope Leo X in 1516, which granted
an indulgence to the dead which could be earned by
those who contributed to the completion of St. Peter's
Basilica in Rome. "Christ never commanded," Luther
wrote angrily to the Archbishop of Mainz, "that indulgences be preached, but he emphatically commanded that the Gospel be preached."

What disturbed Luther was the implication given by
Tetzel that all one needed to do to gain the indulgence
was to give him a donation for the basilica. The Dominican never mentioned confession and renunciation
of sin on the part of the person gaining the indulgence.
In this failure he went far beyond that papal bull,
which gave no sanction to conditionless indulgences.
Tetzel's abuse led Luther to post his 95 theses on a
church door in Wittenberg and the Protestant revolt
was underway.

An indulgence is the remission before God of the

temporal punishment due for sins already forgiven as far as their guilt is concerned. It can be full or partial, accordingly as it removes all or a part of the temporal punishment due for sin. To receive a full (plenary) indulgence, not only must the work to which the indulgence is attached be performed but there must be no attachment to sin. There must also be sacramental confession, reception of the Eucharist, and prayer for the intention of the pope.

The Church's traditional pastoral practice and teaching on indulgences was summed up in a decree of the Council of Trent, dated January 26, 1564. It reads: "Whereas the power of conferring indulgences was granted by Christ to the Church, and she has, even in the most ancient times, used the said power given her by God; the sacred and holy synod teaches and enjoins that the use of indulgences, most salutary for Christian people and approved by the authority of sacred councils, is to be retained in the Church; and it condemns with anathema those who either assert that they are useless, or who deny that there is in the Church the power of granting them."

It is obvious from the very beginning of the Bible that sin brings punishment and must be atoned for either in this life or in the world to come. As Pope Paul VI tells us in his Constitution on Indulgences: "These punishments are imposed by the just and merciful judgment of God for the purification of souls, the defense of the sanctity of the moral order and the restoration of the glory of God to its full majesty" (*Indulgentiarum doctrina*, January 1, 1967).

Many centuries earlier St. Augustine had taught: "Every sin, whether great or small, must be punished either by man himself doing penance, or by God chastising him." All sin is to some degree the rejection of the friendship of God and makes necessary some type of reparation to the majesty of the Creator. It is the teaching of the Church, as the previous chapter established, that this reparation and cleansing of sins which have not made a complete break with God are done in purgatory. It is in purgatory that we find those "who died in the charity of God and truly repentent, but before satisfying with worthy fruits of penance for sins committed and for omissions" (Second Council of Lyons, 1274-1289). As St. James (3:2) reminds us, "For in many things, we all offend." Pope Paul VI sums it up: "All men who walk this earth daily commit at least venial sins; thus all need the mercy of God to be set free from the penal consequences of sin."

The Church's doctrine of the Communion of Saints proclaims a solidarity of mankind and heaven. We are all affected by the acts of others. Jesus suffered for us (1 Pt 2:21), even though He was sinless Himself. Many saints offered their sufferings and trials, not for their own sins, but for the offenses of fellow men and women. As Pope Leo XIII declared in 1902, in his encyclical *Mirae Caritatis*: "For the Communion of Saints is nothing other . . . than the mutual sharing of help, expiation, prayers and benefits among the faithful who, whether they are already in possession of their heavenly fatherland or are detained in purgatory or are still living as pilgrims upon earth, are united and form one commonwealth, whose head is Christ, whose form is charity." This ability to touch one another seems something most people know instinctively; a mother prays for her children, children for their parents.

This doctrine leads to another teaching: the treasury

of the Church. The treasury does not refer to material things — the contents of the Vatican museums or the buildings for worship or schools. It refers to the vast reservoir of merit earned by Jesus, the Virgin Mary, and the saints "offered so that all of mankind could be set free from sin and attain communion with the Father." Over the years the Church has sought ways to apply this boundless treasury to the good of her children. This led to the teaching on indulgences, in some ways an unfortunate word today since it lost its original meaning of forgiveness and has taken on connotations of leniency, self-gratification, prodigality and dissipation. In the minds of many non-Catholics an indulgence is viewed as a permission to sin when the word in its religious sense means just the opposite.

There is one other important argument for the granting of pardon (indulgence), and that rests in the power conferred by Christ on Peter, His vicar on earth, and through him to his successors, the popes. This is the Power of the Keys: "I for my part declare to you, you are 'Rock,' and on this rock I will build my church, and the jaws of death shall not prevail against it. I will entrust to you the keys of the kingdom of heaven. Whatever you declare bound on earth shall be bound in heaven; whatever you declare loosed on earth shall be loosed in heaven" (Mt 16:18-19). In his book *Faith of Millions*, Father John A. O'Brien paraphrased these verses thus: "You are the solid foundation upon which I will build my Church; I assure that the powers of death and evil will not prevail against it. I give you authority to rule the Church, to bind and loosen; to decide what is right and wrong, lawful and unlawful; and your decisions are ratified by God Himself."

Many non-Catholics today affirm that these words were meant only for Peter and ended with him. However, this was not the opinion of the Church down to the time of the Reformation, nor is it the opinion of the Church today. In Peter, Christ was establishing a Church that would endure for all time. In the above words and in many others in Scripture Christ was assuring His followers that both He and the Holy Spirit would be in that Church. Since He intended that Church to continue, He willed that Peter and the Apostles would have successors, thus Peter and the Apostles would pass on to their successors the powers given them by Christ, as necessary for the continuance of what Christ intended.

These two foundations — the Treasury of the Church and the Power of the Keys — are the bases for indulgences. The idea that punishment due sin could be remitted in whole or in part by doing good works was not foreign to the early Church, nor is the idea illogical. The idea that a misdeed can be made up for by doing some family chore exists in most families, and even civil law today often substitutes community service for prison in certain cases. As early as 325, the Council of Nicea recognized that under certain conditions bishops could grant leniency to sinners (Canon 12). Popes, using the Power of the Keys, began decreeing that certain works useful to the common good of the Church could replace penitential practices. When the First Crusade was proclaimed, in 1095, the Council of Clermont ruled that those who from a worthy motive "shall set out to liberate the Church of God in Jerusalem, that journey shall be counted as satisfaction for every penance."

What becomes obvious to anyone who studies Church documentation on indulgences is the care taken and the reasons given. The bull of Clement VI on indulgences, issued in 1325, is an example. After detailing the merits gained by the suffering of Christ, the pope goes on: "Indeed this treasure . . . through blessed Peter, the keeper of the keys of the kingdom of heaven and his successors, his vicars on earth, He has committed to be dispensed for the good of the faithful, both from proper and reasonable causes, now for the whole, now for partial remission of temporal punishment due to sins; in general as in particular (according as they know to be expedient with God), to be applied mercifully to those who truly repentent have confessed.

"Indeed, to the mass of this treasure the merits of the Blessed Mother of God and of all the elect from the first just even to the last, are known to give their help; concerning the consumption of the diminution of this there should be no fear at any time, because of the infinite merits of Christ (as was mentioned before) as well as for the reason that the more are brought to justification by its application, the greater is the increase of the merits themselves."

Pope Paul VI in his 1967 Constitution on Indulgences admits that in the past there have been at times abuses of indulgences. When this has occurred, he says, the Church has moved to correct the situation. It would not serve the People of God to abolish indulgences because they are of benefit to Christian society. "Indeed the faithful," he writes, "when they acquire indulgences understand that by their own powers they could not remedy the harm they have done to themselves and to the entire community by their sin, and they are therefore stirred to salutary humility. Furthermore, the use of indulgences show us how closely we are united to each other in Christ, and how the supernatural life of each can benefit others so that these also may be more easily and more closely united with the Father."

The same Constitution of Pope Paul VI lays down the current norms for indulgences. An indulgence is partial or plenary, according as it removes either part or all of temporal punishment due to sin. Partial indulgences are no longer measured in days and years; the amount of penalty remitted is left to God. Partial and plenary indulgences can always be applied to the dead by way of suffrage; however, neither indulgence can be applied to another living person. To gain an indulgence for oneself it is necessary that one be baptized, not excommunicated, and in the state of grace. A plenary indulgence can be gained only once a day, except one can gain a plenary indulgence at the moment of death even though another has been acquired on that day. A partial indulgence can be gained more than once a day, unless otherwise expressly indicated.

To obtain a plenary indulgence it is necessary to perform the work to which the indulgence is attached and to fulfill the following three conditions: sacramental confession, eucharistic communion, and prayer for the intention of the pope (at least one Our Father and Hail Mary, or any other prayer). It is further required that all attachment to sin, even venial sin, be absent. The three conditions may be fulfilled several days before or after the performance of the work. A single sacramental confession suffices for several plenary indulgences, but Communion must be received and the prayer for the intention of the pope must be undertaken for each indulgence. Where confession or Communion is impossible or very difficult to perform, bishops can dispense these conditions, but there must be the intention of receiving these sacraments as soon as possible.

The decree makes mention of four plenary indulgences that are especially recommended to the faithful and which can be gained every day:

1. Adoration of the Blessed Sacrament for at least one-half hour.

2. Devout reading of Sacred Scriptures for at least one-half hour.

3. The pious exercise of the Way of the Cross.

4. Recitation of the Rosary in a church or public oratory, or in a family group, a religious community or pious association.

There are other particular and special acts or prayers by which the faithful can gain plenary indulgences. The ordinary particular acts include:

Papal Blessing. Granted to the faithful who piously and devoutly receive, even by radio or television, the blessing of the pope imparted to Rome and the world (*urbi et orbi*).

Cemetery Visit. Applicable only to souls in purgatory, this indulgence is granted those who devoutly visit a cemetery and pray, even mentally, for the departed. It may be obtained each day from the first to the eighth of November.

Adoration of the Cross. Granted to the faithful who assist in the solemn liturgy of Good Friday, take part in the adoration and the kissing of the Cross.

Retreat. For those who spend three whole days in the spiritual exercises of a retreat.

Mission. For those who during the time of a parish

mission have heard some of the sermons, and are present at the solemn closing of the mission.

First Communion. For those who receive Communion for the first time, and for those who assist at the ceremonies of First Communion.

First Mass. To the priest who celebrates his First Mass with some solemnity, and to the faithful who devoutly assist at the Mass.

Jubilee. To the priest who on his 25th, 50th and 60th anniversary of his ordination renews before God his resolve to fulfill faithfully the duties of his vocation; to the faithful who assist at his jubilee Mass.

Te Deum. When the hymn is recited publicly on the last day of the year.

Tantum Ergo. Granted on Holy Thursday and Corpus Christi when the Benediction hymn, its versicle and response, and prayer are recited in a solemn manner.

Veni Creator. When the hymn is recited publicly on the first of January and the Feast of Pentecost.

Parochial Church. On its titular feast, and on the second of August when the church is visited and an Our Father and the Creed are recited.

All Souls Day Visit to a Church or Oratory. Applicable only to souls in purgatory and granted to the faithful who on November 2 piously visit a church or oratory and recite the Our Father and Creed. Bishops may transfer this day to the Sunday preceding or following or to All Saints Day.

Renewal of Baptismal Promises. When this is done in the celebration of the Paschal Vigil or on the anniversary of one's baptism.

There are some specialized plenary indulgences:

Patriarchal Basilicas. Granted to the faithful who

visit any of the four Patriarchal Basilicas in Rome and recite one Our Father and the Creed, on the titular feast; on any holy day of obligation; once a year, on any other day of one's choice.

Eucharistic Congress. To the faithful who devoutly participate in the customary solemn eucharistic rite at the close of a Eucharistic Congress.

Moment of Death. To the faithful in danger of death, who cannot be assisted by a priest to bring them the sacraments and impart the Apostolic Blessing with its plenary indulgence, a plenary indulgence to be acquired at the point of death, provided they are properly disposed and have been in the habit of reciting some prayers during their lifetime. The use of a crucifix or cross in gaining this indulgence is praiseworthy. This can be acquired even if another indulgence has been gained on the same day.

Articles of Devotion. Those who devoutly use an article of devotion (crucifix or cross, rosary, scapular or medal) blessed by the pope or any bishop, on the feast of the Holy Apostles Peter and Paul (June 29), provided that they also recite an approved Creed formula.

Diocesan Synod. To the faithful who during the time of a diocesan synod devoutly visit the church in which the synod is meeting, and there recite one Our Father and the Creed.

(Prayers mentioned previously, and other prayers to which plenary indulgences are attached appear in Appendix I.)

As noted earlier, a partial indulgence which remits part of the temporal punishment due sin no longer has any determination of days or years. By the new norms, the faithful who at least with contrite heart perform the action to which a partial indulgence is attached obtain in addition to the remission of temporal punishment acquired by the action itself, an equal remission of punishment through the intervention of the Church. Although the number of prayers and works that can gain an indulgence have been considerably lessened in new norms, there are still too many to be listed here. Those interested in having copies of them can find them in the *Enchiridion of Indulgences* which can be ordered through any Catholic bookstore.

A few other regulations might be mentioned. One does not gain an indulgence automatically but must have at least a general intention of doing so. An indulgence attached to the use of an article of devotion ceases when the article is completely destroyed or sold. When a visit to a church or oratory is required, the visit can be made from noon of the preceding day to midnight of the day itself. To gain an indulgence attached to a prayer, it is sufficient to recite the prayer alternately with a companion or to follow it mentally while it is being recited by another. Those who cannot speak or who cannot hear gain the indulgences attached to public prayers by devoutly raising their minds and affections to God while others are reciting the prayers; for private prayers, it suffices if they recite them mentally or with signs, or if they merely read them with their eyes. Finally, confessors can commute either the prescribed work or conditions for those who because of a legitimate impediment cannot perform the work or fulfill the conditions; this provision is useful to those confined to nursing homes or incapacitated in their own residences.

CHAPTER 11

The End Times

PROBABLY NO OTHER CHRISTIAN TEACHING is surrounded by as much nonsense as is the end of the world. Millenarianism, rapture, Armageddon are but a few of the ideas that have been put forward. Almost from the beginning of Christianity there have been those who, reading the signs of the times, have proclaimed that the end of the world was at hand. These so-called prophets have existed even to our own times. William Miller, the founder of Adventism, concocted a formula from the books of Daniel and Revelation that told him the end of the world was to take place in 1843. When this did not happen, he revised the date to October 22, 1844. Once again his followers sold their belongings, settled their accounts and went outdoors to await the end. When it did not come, disillusionment set in. It took a new prophetess, Ellen White, to revive the movement, but her teachings sensibly were more concerned with health reform and Saturday Sabbath than the date of the millennium. Jehovah's Witnesses have the millennium ending in the year 2914. The elect of the group (144,000 strong) are looking forward to sitting on a hillside watching the last great battle between Jesus, with His angels, and Satan and his followers. Many modern fundamentalist preachers are making fortunes predicting we are in the last days. Others engage in witch-hunts, pointing accusing fingers at various people and movements as being the antichrist.

Judeo-Christian history is one of progression through a series of interventions by God to the ultimate culmination in the day of the Lord. The Prophet Ezekiel wrote (30:2-3): ". . . Thus says the Lord God: Cry, Oh, the day! for near is the day, near is the day of the Lord; a day of clouds, doomsday for the nations shall it be." At first reading this sounds quite dreadful. That is because the word "doom" has taken on the negative connotation of condemnation. In its basic English sense doomsday means only the day of judgment. Doom in its original Anglo-Saxon meaning referred to a law. Doomsday was the day when the law of God would be enforced.

Israel saw the day of the Lord as a fearful one for its enemies but as a day of hope for itself. It is a day of clouds, fire and waste. Panic seizes humanity, which is frightened, filled with confusion. "Disaster upon disaster!" cries out Ezekiel (7:5-9). "See it coming! An end is coming, the end is coming on you. See it coming!. . .Soon now I will pour out my fury upon you and spend my anger upon you; I will judge you according to your conduct, and the consequences of your abominations shall be in your midst; then shall you know that it is I, the Lord, who strike." However, these terrible tribulations apply only to the wicked, for as the Psalmist tells us (34:18): "When the just cry out, the Lord hears them, and from all their distress he rescues them." The Lord will deliver them from death (Ps 33:18) and grant their requests (Ps 20:6).

In the Old Testament all history is directed to this final day. It will mark the end of the world. It is pictured in the Old Testament in militant tones of a great battle between the forces of good and evil. God will enlist the might of nature on His side, striking terror in the enemy's ranks and wiping them out forever. Psalm 98 pictures Yahweh as the victorious king whose "right hand has won victory for him," and the faithful of Israel have seen "the salvation by our God." Beyond the last day, the eschatological theology of the Old Testament is largely undeveloped. It is the New Testament that gives form to Jewish hopes.

In the New Testament the Day of the Lord becomes the Day of Christ. No longer is the promise vague. Jesus announces that the kingdom of heaven has begun and that mankind is in the last days. Certain elements of Old Testament tradition are present: cosmic cataclysms, war, idolatry, judgment. There is not only a promise but an urgency to the coming of the Son of Man in all His glory. It is Jesus who will make the final judgment, after which there will be a new heaven and new earth. The early Christians (including Paul in his first Epistles) did not distinguish between imminence and proximity. They anticipated the Second Coming, or *parousia*, in their own lifetime. While the *parousia* hangs like a cloud over the New Testament, nowhere is its immediacy stated. Instead, Jesus warns that one should always be ready because no one knows the day or the hour.

While *parousia* is a Greek word meaning "coming," its theological sense goes beyond a mere progression or arrival. It is the permanent presence of Christ. In his *Theology of Death*, Karl Rahner says, "It is the fullness and the ending of the history of man

and the world with the glorified humanity of Christ —
now directly manifest in his glory — in God (Mt 24:36;
25:31ff; 1 Thess 5:2; 2 Thess 2:2ff; Rev 20:11ff; 22:17,
20). The resurrection and ascension of Christ and
the sending of the Spirit are the beginning of a process
already irreversible, in which the history of salvation,
mankind's and the individual's, goes on and comes to
an end and fulfillment in what Scripture calls the
parousia." Rahner makes it clear "that history is the
work of God, whose purpose is centered in Jesus
Christ."

The eschatological nature of the New Testament is
sharply delineated in Chapter 24 of Matthew. Unfortunately this chapter has been used over the centuries to establish the proximity of the end of the
world. Many fundamentalist preachers today are using
these same texts to establish that the end is here. They
make selective use of the texts to prove their own pre-
conceptions. However, people should not be misled. In
these same texts Jesus warns of false prophets who
will rise to mislead many. He cautions that in spite of
these signs "the end is not yet near," and again that
these "are the early stages of the birth pangs." It is
vain speculation to attempt to push Scripture beyond
what is there. The teaching of the Church is simple.
Catholics must believe that Christ will return in glory
to judge the living and the dead and that the moment of
this parousia cannot be foretold.

Another subject about which there is much speculation is the nature and person of the antichrist. The only
places in Scripture where the antichrist is specifically
mentioned are four citations in the Epistles of John.
Reflecting the opinion of early Christianity that the
end is near, John writes (1 Jn 2:18), "Children, it is the

final hour; just as you heard that the antichrist was coming, so now many such antichrists have appeared. This makes us certain that it is the final hour." If we take this verse at face value, John seems to expect the almost immediate end of the world, but again we must distinguish between imminence and proximity. By hindsight, we know that the end was not immediate. However, the end is always there before us. The Church interprets this verse in the sense that the final hour means the time between the first and second coming of Christ. It is a fact always before us, even though we do not know when it will happen. It could happen tomorrow, or in a thousand or ten thousand years from now.

The same verse also speaks of not one but many antichrists. John also defines the antichrist in verse 22: "Who is the liar? He who denies that Jesus is the Christ. He is the antichrist, denying the Father and the Son." This does not mean that the notion of antichrist is to be entirely dismissed as irrelevant. Rudolf Pesch believes it still possesses "a vital and urgent relevance." Concerning the question, Karl Rahner has written: "This teaching gives Christians a permanent right not merely to wage war upon anti-Christian powers and ideas in the abstract, but to recognize and flee from men and powers in the concrete as representatives." Thus instead of trying to find and define a particular individual as antichrist, the Church warns us against all movements that are opposed to the way of God. This is in keeping with Mark 13:22. Although the Lord is speaking of the end times, the false prophets and false messiahs of which He speaks belong to every age.

Yet at the same time there is an apocalyptic note to the notion of antichrist, particularly as found in the beast of Revelations and the son of perdition of 2 Thessalonians. The last times are pictured as the struggle of the forces of good and evil. As history approaches its consummation, this warfare becomes more and more intense. However, the antichrist depicted in the final days appears to be Satan himself, knowing that time is running out and being intent to make every gain he can. It is a battle which Christ will win; Satan will be forever vanquished, and the Church militant will disappear to be replaced by the Church triumphant.

It has been suggested by some that the antichrist of Scripture is Satan, and while this cannot be ascertained, it is certain that the devil is an antichrist who has great influence on our last end. One does not hear much these days about Satan and his cohorts, as if he were not a reality. Karl Rahner has written: "The devil . . . is not to be regarded as a mere mythological personification of evil in the world; the existence of the devil cannot be denied." The New Testament portrays Satan as the evil one (Mt 13:19), the enemy (Lk 10:19), the prince of the world (Jn 12:31), a liar and father of lies (Jn 8:44). It was Satan who moved Judas to betray Jesus (Lk 22:3). The devil will continue in the world until vanquished at the end of time. The meaning of all this is contained in 1 Peter 5:8 — "Stay sober and alert. Your opponent the devil is prowling like a roaring lion looking for someone to devour." So while the devil may glory in the modern silence about him, he is an omnipresent force that can affect the salvation of each person.

It is our own salvation that must be of primary concern to us. It may be a popular and titillating sport to speculate on human and cosmological destiny, and while the last days have an ever-present imminence, more proximate and immediately certain is our own demise. At the moment of birth the journey to death begins. The end of the pilgrimage of each human being is drawing close, and at its conclusion a particular judgment will be made of each soul. Pope Benedict XII in 1336 declared solemnly under apostolic authority that the souls of the just promptly after death, or in the case of those who need it, promptly after purification, go to heaven, while those in mortal sin are condemned to hell. Catholics call this the particular judgment to distinguish it from the general judgment which will be made at the end of time. As *The Teaching of Christ* warns us, this judgment should not be looked upon as a judicial procedure; it is something that the individual has already decided by the nature of his or her life; in effect, we make our own judgment. As Paul reminds us, "It is appointed that men die once, and after death be judged" (Heb 9:27). In this judgment is the completion of all that we have striven to be in life — good, bad or indifferent.

There is an old spiritual maxim which says, "As you live, so shall you die." What it means is that if a person habitually lives with sin, he or she will probably die in sin. If a person tries to live according to God, that person will probably die with God. The whole personal thrust of religion is to that last day. Nothing else in the entire world is important — not family, not health, not riches — but how we appear at that final moment when eternal judgment is made. That moment is the fulfillment of all life, for good or for bad. All that we have been in life is added up at that moment. We have written our own tickets to eternal happiness in heaven or to eternal suffering in hell.

"What else, indeed is the judgment, as far as we can grasp it," wrote Bede Jarrett in his *Meditations for Layfolk*, "but the naked setting of our soul as it is now at this moment in the sight of God?" The answer each one of us gives to that question at this moment is a good indication of the answer we will give at the final moment of the last day.

CHAPTER 12

The Day of the Lord

JUDEO-CHRISTIAN HISTORY IS ONE
of progression through various events to the eventual
culmination of the Day of the Lord. The Prophet
Daniel had a view of this cataclysmic event, marking
the reign of Christ. He wrote (7:13, 14): "I saw one like
a son of man coming on the clouds of heaven; when he
reached the Ancient One and was presented before
him, he received dominion, glory and kingship; nations and people of every language serve him. His dominion is an everlasting dominion that shall not be
taken away, his kingship shall not be destroyed."

In His last discourse before His death, Jesus said, "I
am indeed going to prepare a place for you, and then I
shall come back and take you with me, that where I
am you also may be" (Jn 14:3). From the earliest days
of Christianity, the faithful followers of Jesus have
been awaiting His return. The early Christians thought
that the return of the Lord was proximate, and Paul's
two letters to the Thessalonians show how he had to
correct false impressions, yet even Paul himself
thought that the event would occur in his own lifetime
(1 Thess 4:15). Thus from the beginning Christians

have been awaiting what has been variously called the Second Coming, New Advent, New Epiphany, Parousia, or Day of the Lord. Ever since apostolic times there have been those who have been predicting that the end is at hand.

It is almost common teaching among modern fundamentalists that we are in the last days. They point to famine, pestilence and earthquakes to show that the words in the twenty-fourth chapter of Matthew are being fulfilled, that the wars which wrack the world are proof that the birth pangs have begun. The fundamentalist script runs something like this: we are in the last days because the biblical signs are being fulfilled. There is an increase in wars (Dan 9:26, Mt 24:6). Materialism has become rampant (2 Tim 3:1-5). Christianity is being denied (2 Jn 7-11) and ridiculed (Jude 17-19). Christians are being persecuted for their beliefs (Mt 24:9).

The purported signs could go on and on. All of these signs, they say, mean that the decisive day is at hand. First there will be seven days of tribulation. Then a trumpet sound will blast the earth and Jesus with His host of angels will come on the clouds. The faithful remnant will be seized up to meet Him (the rapture). The battle of Armageddon will be won by the hosts of the Lord. Jesus will go to Jerusalem and take His seat on the throne of David, where with the saints He will establish the thousand-year rule of God (the millennium) on the earth.

This apocalyptic preaching is heard daily through radio and television as the fundamentalist preachers send forth their message of impending doom. The position of the Church on all this is that while Scripture gives some clues, we must be careful and not push

Scripture too far. As pointed out earlier, only two things are certain: (1) Christ will come again as king and judge; (2) but no one knows when the coming will take place, hence we must always be prepared. All the rest is open to interpretations. We do know, however, the Second Coming will mark the end of time, when Christ, having destroyed the enemies of God, will turn the kingdom over to the Father (1 Cor 15:24). This kingdom will belong eternally to the Father and Christ (Rev 11:15). Those who have been faithful to Christ will be with Him forever, seeing Him as He is (1 Jn 3:2), and reigning with him forever and ever (Rev 22:5).

However, before that triumphant time, first must come the resurrection of the body and the general judgment. Paul envisions the Second Coming and the resurrection taking place almost together (1 Thess 4:16). Jesus describes Himself as "coming in the clouds with great power and glory." He will dispatch His angels and assemble His chosen from the four winds, from the farthest bounds of earth and sky (Mk 13:26-27). What rises up is a complete person to a new and more wonderful life. Job's hope (20:25) finds meaning: "I know that my Redeemer lives, and that he will at the last stand forth upon the dust; whom I myself shall see: my own eyes, not another's, shall behold him; and from my flesh I shall see God."

Belief in the resurrection of the body is Catholic dogma, repeated each Sunday in the recitation of the Creed at Mass. Lazarus coming forth from the tomb at Christ's command is proof of His promise "I am the resurrection and the life: whoever believes in me, though he should die, will come to life" (Jn 11:25-26). In contrast to the Greek concept of only the soul going on to immortality, the Christian teaching is that the whole person — body and soul — shall be restored. The resurrection of the body was very meaningful to Paul and he frequently considers it, making an extended treatment of the subject (1 Cor 15). Paul paraphrases Isaiah (Eph 5:14): "Awake, O sleeper, arise from the dead, and Christ will give you light." This radical teaching, that death is not an end but a passage of the total being to eternal life, is at the root of Christianity.

Paul describes the resurrected body as incorruptible, glorious, strong and spiritual (1 Cor 15:42-44). St. Thomas Aquinas ponders these verses at length in the *Summa Theologica*, and restates Paul to say that the risen body will possess impassibility, subtlety, agility and clarity. Since St. Paul tells us (1 Cor 15:42) that the risen body will be incorruptible, it must therefore be impassible, free from immoderate movements of the heart, not subject to pain. "The human body," says Aquinas, "and all that it contains will be perfectly subject to the rational soul, even as the soul will be perfectly subject to God. Wherefore it will be impossible for the glorified body to be subject to any change contrary to the disposition whereby it is perfected by the soul." Subtlety is the power to penetrate; it is a quality of a spiritual body. This does not mean that the risen one is a spirit, for a spirit lacks a body. Sun passing through a glass window to fill a room is a likeness of subtlety.

The risen body will be agile, that is, capable of movement. St. Thomas also adds swiftness of motion to the notion of agility. He writes: "Since, after the resurrection, the soul will perfectly dominate the body, both on account of the perfection of its own power, and on account of the glorified body's aptitude resulting from the outflow of glory it receives from the soul, there will be no labor in the saints' movements, and thus it may be said that the bodies of the saints will be agile." The final quality Aquinas assigns to the glorified body is clarity, or refulgence and lightsomeness, which "will result from the overflow of the soul's glory into the body." This is what Jesus meant when He said: "The saints will shine like the sun in their Father's kingdom" (Mt 13:43). An example of this risen glory is given in the Transfiguration of Jesus (Mt 17:2): "He was transfigured before their eyes. His face became as dazzling as the sun, his clothes as radiant as light."

A study of the resurrected Christ gives us an indication of what we shall be like after our own resurrections. Our bodies will be restored in their entirety and reunited with our souls. We will be the same, yet different. It was this difference that made immediate recognition of Jesus difficult for Mary Magdalene after the Resurrection. The disciples on the road to Emmaus and the fishing disciples in Galilee had this same problem. Mary recognized Jesus by His voice and the Emmaus disciples by His actions. The risen body will be able to pass thrugh solid objects as Jesus did when entering the locked room where the Apostles hid after the crucifixion. Yet this same body will be palpable, able to be felt. As Jesus told the Apostles (Lk 24:39): "Touch me, and see that a ghost does not have flesh and bones as I do." As St. Gregory says, "Our Lord offered His flesh to be handled, which He had brought in through the closed doors, so as to afford a complete proof that after His resurrection His body was unchanged in nature though changed in glory." Another quality the glorified body will have is its ability to rise, unaffected by gravity. The Gospel of Luke describes Jesus' ascension as being "taken up to heaven" (Lk 24:51), but His rising was by His own power. St. Thomas also proposes that since the glorified body will be in complete obedience to the will, it will be able to appear and disappear at will. He gives the example of Christ, who vanished from the sight of the disciples at Emmaus.

Not only the saved but also the damned will rise at the resurrection; this is clear from Matthew 25. They will be punished both in soul and body. Thus the bodies of the damned will be incorruptible, for the withdrawal of death will lead to everlasting punishment which the damned have been promised. Since the damned will be capable of suffering, their bodies will also be passible (capable of feeling and suffering). The damned will also be locked into an evil will, the state in which each died. Scripture does not make clear when the damned will rise, but it will have to be before the final judgment.

Jesus in a discourse to the Jews (Jn 5) told them that He was to be the principle of resurrection and judgment. At His voice the dead will rise, and those whose lives were worthy will go to eternal life and the evil doers to condemnation. Jesus more clearly spells out this judgment in Matthew 25:31-46. Here the Son of Man, seated on a throne, surrounded by angels, will render judgment on all who have ever lived, basing the judgment on actions done and actions omitted. There is a social character to the judgment for it is rooted in how we have treated our neighbor, with neighbor being defined by His parable of the Good Samaritan.

In the Old Testament God's judgment was a continuing act. God judged the sin of Adam and Eve. He passed sentence on Cain. It was God's judgment of humanity that brought on the flood. The plagues and the Exodus resulted from God's judgment on Egypt. In the desert God made judgments on Israel and even Moses. The Bible explains the catastrophes that befell mankind as happening because of God's judgment of humanity's failures. The judgment of God hung like a threat over human history. As the Bible developed, so also did the notion of another judgment, an eschatological judgment. This notion was strongly advanced by the prophets, particularly Isaiah, Amos, Ezekiel and Daniel. The Psalmist frequently prays to be spared the wrath of God's judgment, believing that since all are sinners, none can escape the wrath of God's justice except through His mercy.

Thus the notion of a final judgment was well established when Jesus appeared on the scene. The preaching of the Baptist was a powerful statement for the need of reform to escape the "unquenchable fire" (Mt 3:7-12). Judgment is a repeated theme in the teaching of Jesus, and this is particularly stressed in the Gospel of John: "The Father has given over to him power to pass judgment because he is son of Man; no need for you to be surprised at this, for an hour is coming in which all those in their tombs shall hear his voice and come forth. Those who have done right shall rise to live; the evildoers shall rise to be damned" (Jn 5:27-29). Jesus has come to heal and save from adverse judgment, but there are those who have given themselves to the prince of the world and who will be lost.

For Catholics, belief in the last judgment is a dogmatic necessity. Its existence is stated in both the Apostles' and Nicene Creeds. Jesus' discourse on the last judgment (Mt 25) is one that deserves study. After speaking of the end of the world, and the signs accompanying it, and after warning that the exact time is hidden and all must therefore be ever ready, Jesus tells two parables. The first parable of the ten virgins stresses the point of eternal vigilance. The second parable of the silver pieces given to three different servants rebukes negligence and omission. Then immediately Jesus describes the last judgment: His coming to the royal throne in glory, His separation of the people of the nations into sheep and goats, at the end of which all humans will go off to eternal punishment or eternal life. Identifying human needs with Himself, Jesus makes His judgment on how each has reacted to those who have touched their lives. In this judgment we are judged as members of society. Love is the key to the last judgment, just as it is the key to the very nature of God.

Father John A. Hardon, S.J., in *The Catholic Catechism* brings out a point about the last judgment that is often forgotten, namely, that we will also be judged on things that happen after we are dead. He writes: "There is a deeper reason for the final judgment, arising from the nature of human acts. Their full import cannot be gauged the moment they are done, or even at the end of the life of a person who does them.

"Things in a process of change are not fit subjects for judgment before they have come to a stop. No act can be fully assessed before it is finished and its results are evident. What may seem profitable at first may turn out to be damaging.

"All the same, though a person's career ends with death, his life still goes on in a sense, and is affected by what happens afterward. He lives on in people's memories, and his reputation, good or bad, may not correspond to his real character. He lives on also in his children who are, so to speak, part of their parents. "But most important, a person survives in the results of his actions. Unkindness does not stop with an act of impatience or spite; its effects continue in a never-ending spiral long after the sin was committed. . . . All these are submitted to divine scrutiny the moment a person enters eternity, but a full and public verdict cannot be pronounced while time rolls on in its course. Only on the last day, when everything we have done will have reached its end result, can a truly final judgment be made."

Therefore, in the words of the breviary hymn:

> Prepare us for that day of days
> When Christ from heaven will come with might
> To call us out of dust again,
> Our bodies glorified in light.

After the judgment only one thing remains: the creation of a new heaven and earth. Isaiah (65:17) wrote: "Lo, I am about to create new heavens and a new earth; the things of the past shall not be remembered. . . ." The Book of Revelation (21:1-4) gives us a similar thought: "Then I saw new heavens and a new earth. The former heavens and the former earth had passed away, and the sea was no longer. I also saw a new Jerusalem, the holy city, coming down out of heaven from God, beautiful as a bride prepared to meet her husband. I heard a loud voice from the throne cry out: 'This is God's dwelling among men. He shall dwell with them and they shall be his people and he shall be their God who is always with them. He shall wipe every tear from their eyes, and there shall be no more death or mourning, crying out or pain, for the former world has passed away!' "

So be it. *Maranatha!*

Come, Lord Jesus!

APPENDIX I

Prayers Having a Plenary Indulgence

Look down upon me, good and gentle Jesus
(En ego, o bone et dulcissime Jesu)

Look down upon me, good and gentle Jesus, while before your face I humbly kneel, and with burning soul pray and beseech you to fix deep in my heart lively sentiments of faith, hope and charity, true contrition for my sins, and a firm purpose of amendment, while I contemplate with great love and tender pity your five wounds, pondering over them within me, calling to mind the words which David, your prophet, said of you, my good Jesus: "They have pierced my hands and my feet; they have numbered all my bones" (Ps 21, 17-18).

A plenary indulgence is granted on each Friday of Lent and Passiontide to the faithful who after Communion piously recite the above prayer before an image of Christ crucified; on other days of the year the indulgence is partial.

106

Most sweet Jesus — Act of Reparation
(Jesu dulcissime — Reparationis actus)

Most sweet Jesus, whose overflowing charity for men is requited by so much forgetfulness, negligence and contempt, behold us prostrate before you, eager to repair by a special act of homage the cruel indifference and injuries to which your loving Heart is everywhere subject.

Mindful, alas! that we ourselves have had a share in such great indignities, which we now deplore from the depths of our hearts, we humbly ask your pardon and declare our readiness to atone by voluntary expiation, not only for our own personal offenses, but also for the sins of those, who, straying far from the path of salvation, refuse in their obstinate infidelity to follow you, their Shepherd and Leader, or, renouncing the promises of their baptism, have cast off the sweet yoke of your law.

We are now resolved to expiate each and every deplorable outrage committed against you; we are now determined to make amends for the manifold offenses against Christian modesty in unbecoming dress and behavior, for all the foul seductions laid to ensnare the feet of the innocent, for the frequent violations of Sundays and holydays, and the shocking blasphemies uttered against you and your Saints. We wish also to make amends for the insults to which your Vicar on earth and your priests are subjected, for the profanation, by conscious neglect or terrible acts of sacrilege, of the very Sacrament of your divine love, and lastly for the public crimes of nations who resist the rights and teaching authority of the Church which you have founded.

Would that we were able to wash away such abominations with our blood. We now offer, in reparation for these violations of your divine honor, the satisfaction you once made to your Eternal Father on the cross and which you continue to renew daily on our altars; we offer it in union with the acts of atonement of your Virgin Mother and all the Saints and of the pious faithful on earth; and we sincerely promise to make recompense, as far as we can with the help of your grace, for all neglect of your great love and for the sins we and others have committed in the past. Henceforth, we will live a life of unswerving faith, of purity of conduct, of perfect observance of the precepts of the Gospel and especially that of charity. We promise to the best of our power to prevent others from offending you and to bring as many as possible to follow you.

O loving Jesus, through the intercession of the Blessed Virgin Mother, our model in reparation, deign to receive the voluntary offering we make of this act of expiation; and by the crowning gift of perseverance keep us faithful unto death in our duty and the allegiance we owe to you, so that we may all one day come to that happy home, where with the Father and the Holy Spirit you live and reign, God, forever and ever. Amen.

A partial indulgence is granted to the faithful who piously recite the above act of reparation. A plenary indulgence is granted if it is publicly recited on the feast of the Most Sacred Heart of Jesus.

Most sweet Jesus, Redeemer — Act of Dedication of the Human Race to Jesus Christ the King
(Jesu dulcissime, Redemptor)

Most sweet Jesus, Redeemer of the human race, look down upon us humbly prostrate before you. We are yours, and yours we wish to be; but to be more surely united with you, behold each one of us freely consecrates himself today to your Most Sacred Heart. Many indeed have never known you; many, too, despising your precepts, have rejected you. Have mercy on them all, most merciful Jesus, and draw them to your Sacred Heart.

Be King, O Lord, not only to the faithful who have never forsaken you, but also to the prodigal children who have abandoned you; grant that they may quickly return to their Father's house, lest they die of wretchedness and hunger.

Be King of those who are deceived by erroneous opinions, or whom discord keeps aloof, and call them back to the harbor of truth and the unity of faith, so that soon there may be but one flock and one Shepherd.

Grant, O Lord, to your Church assurance of freedom and immunity from harm; give tranquillity of order to all nations; make the earth resound from pole to pole with one cry: Praise to the divine Heart that wrought our salvation; to it be glory and honor for ever. Amen.

A partial indulgence is granted to the faithful who piously recite the above Act of Dedication of the Human Race to Jesus Christ the King. A plenary indulgence is granted, if it is recited publicly on the feast of our Lord Jesus Christ the King.

Down in adoration falling
(Tantum ergo)

Down in adoration falling,
Lo! the sacred Host we hail;
Lo! o'er ancient forms departing,
Newer rites of grace prevail;
Faith for all defects supplying,
Where the feeble senses fail.

To the everlasting Father,
And the Son who reigns on high,
With the Holy Spirit proceeding
Forth from each eternally,
Be salvation, honor, blessing,
Might and endless majesty. Amen.

V. You have given them bread from heaven,
R. Having all sweetness within it.

Let us pray. O God, who in this wonderful Sacrament left us a memorial of your Passion: grant, we implore you, that we may so venerate the sacred mysteries of your Body and Blood, as always to be conscious of the fruit of your Redemption. You who live and reign forever and ever. Amen.

(Roman Breviary)

A partial indulgence is granted to the faithful who devoutly recite the above strophes. But a plenary indulgence is granted on Holy Thursday and on the feast of Corpus Christi, if they are recited in a solemn manner.

The Te Deum
(Te Deum)

O God, we praise you, and acknowledge you to be the
    supreme Lord.
Everlasting Father, all the earth worships you.
All the Angels, the heavens and all angelic powers,
All the Cherubim and Seraphim, continuously cry to
    you:
Holy, holy, holy, Lord God of Hosts!
Heaven and earth are full of the Majesty of your glory.
The glorious choir of the Apostles,
The wonderful company of Prophets,
The white-robed army of Martyrs, praise you.
Holy Church throughout the world acknowledges you:
The Father of infinite Majesty;
Your adorable, true and only Son;
Also the Holy Spirit, the Comforter.
O Christ, you are the King of glory!
You are the everlasting Son of the Father.
When you took it upon yourself to deliver man,
You did not disdain the Virgin's womb.
Having overcome the sting of death, you opened the
    Kingdom of Heaven to all believers.
You sit at the right hand of God in the glory of the
    Father.
We believe that you will come to be our judge.
We, therefore, beg you to help your servants whom you
    have redeemed with your Precious Blood.
Let them be numbered with your Saints in everlasting
    glory.

Save your people, O Lord, and bless your inheritance!
Govern them, and raise them up forever.
Every day we thank you.
And we praise your Name forever; yes, forever and
  ever.
O Lord, deign to keep us from sin this day.
Have mercy on us, O Lord, have mercy on us.
Let your mercy, O Lord, be upon us, for we have hoped
  in you.
O Lord, in you I have put my trust; let me never be put
  to shame.

*A partial indulgence is granted to the faithful
who recite the Te Deum in thanksgiving. But a
plenary indulgence is granted, if the hymn is recited publicly on the last day of the year.*

Come, Holy Spirit, Creator blest
(Veni, Creator)

Come, Holy Spirit, Creator blest,
And in our souls take up your rest;
Come with your grace and heavenly aid
To fill the hearts which you have made.

O Comforter, to you we cry,
O heavenly gift of God Most High,
O fount of life and fire of love,
And sweet anointing from above.

You in your sevenfold gifts are known;
You, finger of God's hand we own;
You, promise of the Father, you
Who do the tongue with power imbue.

Kindle our senses from above,
And make our hearts o'erflow with love;
With patience firm and virtue high
The weakness of our flesh supply.

Far from us drive the foe we dread,
And grant us your peace instead;
So shall we not, with you for guide,
Turn from the path of life aside.

Oh, may your grace on us bestow
The Father and the Son to know;
And you, through endless times confessed,
Of both the eternal Spirit blest.

Now to the Father and the Son,
Who rose from death, be glory given,
With you, O holy Comforter,
Henceforth by all in earth and heaven. Amen.

A partial indulgence is granted to the faithful who devoutly recite the hymn Come, Holy Spirit, Creator blest. But a plenary indulgence is granted, if the hymn is recited publicly on the first of January and on the feast of Pentecost.

Renewal of Baptismal Promises

I., N.N., who through the tender mercy of the Eternal Father was privileged to be baptized "in the name of the Lord Jesus" (Acts 19, 5) and thus to share in the dignity of his divine Sonship, wish now in the presence of this same loving Father and of his only-begotten Son to renew in all sincerity the promises I solemnly made at the time of my holy Baptism.

I, therefore, now do once again renounce Satan; I renounce all his works; I renounce all his allurements. I believe in God, the Father almighty, Creator of heaven and earth. I believe in Jesus Christ, his only Son, our Lord, who was born into this world and who suffered and died for my sins and rose again. I believe in the Holy Spirit, the Holy Catholic Church, the communion of Saints, the forgiveness of sins, the resurrection of the body and life everlasting.

Having been buried with Christ unto death and raised up with him unto a new life, I promise to live no longer for myself or for that world which is the enemy of God but for him who died for me and rose again, serving God, my heavenly Father, faithfully and unto death in the holy Catholic Church.

Taught by our Savior's command and formed by the word of God, I now dare to say:

Our Father, who art in heaven, hallowed be thy name; thy kingdom come; thy will be done on earth as it is in heaven. Give us this day our daily bread; and forgive us our trespasses as we forgive those who trespass against us; and lead us not into temptation, but deliver us from evil. Amen.

A partial indulgence is granted to the faithful who renew their baptismal promises according to any formula in use; but a plenary indulgence is granted, if this is done in the celebration of the Paschal Vigil or on the anniversary of one's baptism.

Exercise of the Way of the Cross
(Viae Crucis exercitium)

A plenary indulgence is granted to the faithful who make the pious exercise of the Way of the Cross.

In the pious exercise of the *Way of the Cross* we recall anew the sufferings, which the divine Redeemer endured, while going from the praetorium of Pilate, where he was condemned to death, to the mount of Calvary, where he died on the cross for our salvation.

The gaining of the plenary indulgence is regulated by the following norms:

(1) The pious exercise must be made before stations of the *Way of the Cross* legitimately erected.

(2) For the erection of the *Way of the Cross* fourteen crosses are required, to which it is customary to add fourteen pictures or images, which represent the stations of Jerusalem.

(3) According to the more common practice, the pious exercise consists of fourteen pious readings, to which some vocal prayers are added. However, nothing more is required than a pious meditation on the Passion and Death of the Lord, which need not be a particular consideration of the individual mysteries of the stations.

(4) A movement from one station to the next is required.

But if the pious exercise is made publicly and if it is not possible for all taking part to go in an orderly way from station to station, it suffices if at least the one conducting the exercise goes from station to station, the others remaining in their place.

Those who are "impeded" can gain the same indulgence, if they spend at least one half hour in pious reading and meditation on the Passion and Death of our Lord Jesus Christ.

For those belonging to Oriental rites, among whom this pious exercise is not practiced, the respective Patriarchs can determine some other pious exercise in memory of the Passion and Death of our Lord Jesus Christ for the gaining of this indulgence.

APPENDIX II

Limbo

The word limbo comes from the Latin *limbus*, meaning an edge, border or hem. The word was not used by the early Church Fathers, nor is it found in Scripture. The word was in general use at the time of St. Thomas Aquinas and he discusses it in seven articles in his *Summa Theologica*. The word has a double connotation. First, there is limbo of the fathers, the hell of the Creed. The second usage refers to the limbo of infants, the place where unbaptized children go.

In its first usage it means the place where those who died before the redemption of Christ and who did not deserve hell went to await the time when the gates of heaven would be reopened. Limbo of the fathers had its origin in the Jewish idea of sheol where as the Douai-Rheims text said, "a house is appointed to everyone that liveth" (Job 30:23). It was this state that Jesus referred to as Abraham's bosom (Lk 16:22). By the sin of Adam heaven was closed to mankind. Yet there were many virtuous people who believed in God and served Him. These souls did not deserve eternal death. Hence they awaited the day when they could be

117

joined to God. That day came when Jesus died and reunited mankind to God. Before His resurrection, Jesus went to these souls and led them to heaven. This limbo ceased to exist after the resurrection.

The limbo of infants is a state of rest and natural happiness to which unbaptized children go. This state has never been defined by the Church and one is free to believe or disbelieve in its existence. It developed from the logic of theologians. One of the most important texts in the theology of baptism is John 3:5 where Jesus tells Nicodemus that no one can enter God's kingdom without baptism. The Church teaches that there are three kinds of baptism: baptism of water, that is, baptism as we commonly know it; baptism of blood, that is, martyrdom for the Christian faith or Christian virtue; and baptism of desire, that is, an implicit desire of baptism by desiring to do the will of God (if one knew God wanted baptism of water, one would seek it). Since baptism of desire requires the use of reason, this baptism is not possible for children below the age of reason. Therefore, argued the theologians, children who died before the use of reason do not deserve hell, they cannot go to heaven unless baptized, hence they go to a place called limbo.

The early Church did not seem too concerned with this subject. Innocent III in 1206 distinguished between lack of baptism and actual sin; the first deprived of the vision of God but the latter caused actual torment. The Second Council of Lyons (1274) and the Council of Florence (1439) likewise saw different punishments. However, neither of these councils mentioned limbo or specifically considered infants dying before baptism. The rigid Jansenists taught that the unbaptized went to hell and accused the defenders of limbo as being heretics.

Pope Pius VI in 1794 through the only Church doctrine that mentions the limbo of children condemned this Jansenist theory.

Since the time of Pius VI's condemnation, no responsible theologians have asserted that unbaptized infants have gone to hell. In its place have developed various salvation theories which attempt to reconcile the necessity of baptism with God's salvific will. These various theories are still under debate; nevertheless, the Holy See has continually warned against the delay of infant baptism. Some argue that the Church is merely following the safer course but a study of Church documents would seem to go beyond this opinion. Vatican Council II in its *Dogmatic Constitution on the Church* (14) asserts that the Church is necessary for salvation and that Christ Himself "explicitly asserted the necessity of faith and baptism."

Since the matter of limbo has not been closed by the Church, speculation will continue. Some modern theologians propose a special type of baptism of desire that would belong to the innocence of childhood and appeal to the growing tradition on the salvation of such children. It is even argued by some that the Church through the Power of the Keys can rule in favor of children dying without baptism before the use of reason. However, the Holy See has made no comment on any of these opinions, allowing the debate to continue and clarify.

Good pastoral procedures would require the absence of polemics or extremes on the subject. Pastors, following the direction of the magisterium, must continue to insist on the prompt baptism of infants. Special sensitivity must be shown to those parents whose children have died without baptism. The theologian

Peter Gumpel has written on this subject that parents should be told "that there is no definite doctrine of faith regarding the fate of such children, and that consequently they can entrust the final lot of their child to the mysterious but infinitely kind and powerful love of God, to whose grace no limit is set by the earthly circumstances which He in His providence has allowed to come about."

One last subject of current concern is the fate of aborted infants whose number increases annually and in many places exceeds the number of live births. An article in a popular Catholic publication proposed their salvation, basing its argument on a species of baptism of blood. "They died," said the article, "because of the sin of others and give mute witness to God's creation and the sanctity of life. It is difficult to see how God's mercy and saving love can be satisfied by the separation of these souls who committed no sin of their own and who left this world because of the selfishness of another." Thus a whole new avenue of speculation is opened on a question that is far from settled.

APPENDIX III

Common Questions
and Their Answers

Angels

*A priest gave a Sunday homily in which he said
that there are no such things as angels, and that
when the Bible mentions them it merely means
an inspiration that comes from God — like a
thought. Is he right?*

No, he is not. Angels are mentioned in the Bible
from Genesis on, sometimes in human form as in the
cases of Lot and Tobias. The New Testament specifically names angels appearing to Mary, to minister to
Christ, at His tomb, and so forth. Our doctrine of the
Guardian Angel evolved from Raphael's care of and
words to Tobias. There is nothing illogical about
angels or the biblical fact that they act so often as
messengers of God. If you understood the priest cor-
rectly, he is going completely against biblical tradition
and scholarship. Moreover, Vatican Council II documents speak frequently of angels.

Anointing of the Sick

My mother was a fallen-away Catholic. She passed away suddenly in a Catholic hospital. The chaplain, there, assured me that he would anoint her and I am sure this was done, probably after death. Since then I have been deeply disturbed. My mother was a good woman, though not religious. Did the anointing do her any good? Would it remove sins, even mortal sins? Would the fact that it was given after death make a difference? Is an anointing the same thing as receiving Extreme Unction?

Extreme Unction is now called Anointing of the Sick. It is a sacrament for those seriously ill or in danger of death from age or some other cause. It may be administered more than once, and the name was changed to indicate that it is not meant solely for those on the brink of death. It may be administered conditionally even after apparent death, and this is probably what was done in the case of your mother. However, it has no effect if the person is already dead. The sacrament confers grace, the remission of venial sins and inculpably unconfessed mortal sins. You should not be troubled. Spiritually, you did all that you could for your mother. For the rest, you must leave her to the mercy of God who is a loving Father who wants none of His children to be lost. He alone can read your mother's heart and know what goodness and love were there. Christ's description of the Last Judgment (Mt 25:31-46) is not a legalistic one. He is concerned about our relationship with others and our fulfillment of the Golden Rule. Pray for your mother and put yor confidence in God's mercy and justice.

Antichrist

Would you give me your opinion, and state the Church's teaching on the antichrist? Until recently I didn't know what he was going to be like, or what to look for. My non-Catholic friends seem to know and think it will be easy for persons to be misled. Maybe I have made the mistake of thinking that the antichrist wouldn't emerge during my lifetime, but after viewing TV and movie film fare I have been wondering.

All we know with certainty is that the end of the world is coming, and that before it does the antichrist will appear. Christ told us that since no one knew the day or the hour but the Father, we should always be ready. Fundamentalist Protestants make the mistake of interpreting dates and making predictions, none of which have been accurate. The trouble with the film scenarios that you mentioned is that they upset one's faith and foster superstition. If we are ready to meet Christ at any moment, we do not have to worry about the end of the world.

Apocalyptic Age

Speaking for a number of relatives, friends and myself, we have come to believe that we may be living in the time of St. Paul's "Great Apostasy." To avoid the error of private interpretation of Scripture, we would like to know what the authoritative teaching of the Church is on this matter. To us it is becoming evident that the pieces are falling into place with increasing rapidity, and we would like to be certain that it is proper to hold this opinion.

Although Christ predicted the end of the world and His second coming; and, although Paul and John repeatedly refer to these facts, the Church's position is contained in Christ's own words: "You know not the day nor the hour." Christ predicted both the end of the world and the fall of Jerusalem, and sometimes these predictions are mixed and confused by people. Many people believe we are entering the Apocalyptic Age. Some Protestant groups are firm believers in this fact. However, there have been ages past when men thought that the conditions were present for the end of the world and it never came about. It is Christian teaching that we should always be prepared because if the end of the world does not come in its totality immediately, it does come almost immediately in our own death of which also we do not know "the day nor the hour."

Archangels

While reading Tobit, I came across this verse: "I am the Angel Raphael, one of the seven who stand before the throne of God." Holy Scripture gives the names of (as far as I can find) only three angels: Michael, Gabriel and Raphael. Is there any information that might reveal the names of the other four?

The reference in Tobit (12:15) and another in Revelation (1:4) speak of seven angels who stand before God's throne. These seven angels are called archangels because of their proximity to God. The Bible only lists the three you mention but Jewish tradition names the others as Uriel, Raguel, Sarakiel and Jeremiel.

Baptism, Cesarean

Would you please advise regarding this case? A pregnant mother dies on an operating table. Should there be an immediate operation to have a cesarean section so that the child could be baptized?

Yes. If the fetus is viable there should be an attempt made to save the child's life. If not viable (incapable of sustaining life outside the womb), there is a grave obligation to have a cesarean section in order to baptize the child. However, if there is moral certitude on the part of the doctor that the infant is dead, this obligation does not bind. The same method of baptism should be used here as when baptizing an embryo in a miscarriage.

Body Donation

I would like to give my body to science (Indiana University Medical School). As a Catholic what must I do?

This question is coming up more frequently and many Catholics have the idea that it is forbidden. Pope Pius XII specifically stated that such action was not forbidden Catholics, adding: "A person may will to dispose of his body and to destine it to ends that are useful, morally irreproachable and even noble, among them the desire to aid the sick and suffering." The important thing is that all arrangements should be made beforehand and the person who is to handle your estate be aware of them. A legal form separate from a will (which involves probate delays) should be drawn up. Write a letter to the dean of the Indiana University Medical School (1100 W. Michigan St., Indianapolis, IN 46202) for proper legal forms and all necessary instructions.

Burial

A friend and I were talking about the rules for burial in the Church but we disagreed on one thing. I say when placing the corpse in the grave, it is put in facing west to the setting sun. My friend thinks it faces east. Who is right?

I am afraid you lose this one. The early Christian practice, still followed in many places today, is to place the corpse facing east so that it will be looking toward the Parousia, or second coming of Christ, which is expected to take place from the east.

Candle at Wake

What is the significance of placing a lighted candle at a casket during the "viewing" period in a funeral parlor?

It is a symbol of resurrection, probably derived from the paschal candle. Candles developed from the catacombs where they were used to illuminate the darkness. At that time also, Roman officials were flanked by candles to indicate their importance. When the Church emerged from the catacombs, candles continued to be used at the altar to indicate a place of importance and were thus adapted for general liturgical use. Then the large paschal candle was introduced into the liturgy. It was lighted at the Easter Vigil during the Exsultet from the new fire and was a symbol of the resurrection of Christ, the Light of the World. In some areas the custom developed of placing one or several candles at the bier as reminders of the promise of resurrection.

Cemeteries

In a parish bulletin the Chancery reminded parishioners that as a general rule no Catholic may be buried in other than a Catholic cemetery. This is spiritual blackmail. It seems to me that the hierarchy politicians are more interested in selling a plot of ground to put a body in after the soul has left than in saving a soul in a body that is walking around.

The early Church, as testified by the catacombs, showed great reverence for those who "fell asleep in the Lord." Since that time the Church has taught that the body of a Christian, which is a temple of the Holy Spirit and a tabernacle of the Eucharist, be honorably buried in a safe and becoming place. Canon Law (1204) states that this should be consecrated ground set aside by the authority of the bishop. It is so sacred that certain classes are forbidden Christian burial in such a place, such as notorious apostates, the excommunicated, and other "public and manifest sinners." Bodies of the faithful should be buried in consecrated ground (1205). Every parish, if possible, should have its own cemetery (1208), and where this is not possible several should join together. If possible, there should be a separate enclosed place, nonconsecrated, for those to whom ecclesiastical burial is denied. The cemetery should be carefuly guarded and protected (1210). The Third Council of Baltimore ruled that money from the sale of plots should be used for the upkeep of the cemetery; if there are surplus funds, they are to be used for religious and charitable purposes as directed by the ordinary (bishop).

Communion of Saints

Would you please explain the phrase "communion of saints" as used in the Apostles' Creed? I always thought it meant sharing in the merits of the saints since they by their holy lives stored up merits in heaven.

You are correct in your understanding except that you do not go far enough. It is the sharing of spiritual goods between the Church Militant (we on earth), the Church Suffering (those in purgatory), and the Church Triumphant (the angels and saints in heaven). It is more than just our sharing in the merits of the saints. Each of the divisions can pray for the other two and we can share our own merits (through indulgences, etc.) with those in purgatory, thus helping to shorten their stay in purgatory.

Cremation

I was informed by a priest that Pope John XXIII approved cremation. I inquired further of other priests and they were evasive, saying they didn't know or were not sure. I personally think cremation is a step forward.

There is a difference between "approved" and "permitted." I don't think it was exact to say Pope

John XXIII approved cremation. In 1886 the Holy Office issued a decree forbidding cremation because it was used by the anticlerical movement as a sign of contempt for the Church and a denial of the doctrine of the resurrection. This decree was carried over into the Canon Law revision of 1917. On May 8, 1963, the Congregation for the Doctrine of the Faith (successor of the Holy Office) issued a declaration modifying the Church's ban. Cremation is now permitted for a serious private or public reason, as long as it does not involve contempt for the Church or its teachings. A person who decides to be cremated may receive the last rites and be given ecclesiastical burial. A priest may go to the crematorium to say prayers for the deceased but full liturgical ceremonies are not permitted there. Recently a veteran missioner died in the United States after a long illness. In his will he asked to be cremated and his ashes sent to Japan for interment. His superiors followed his wishes. Cremation is the custom in Japan, even for Catholics. A Catholic desiring to be cremated would do well to make arrangements in advance, including the funeral services, so that there will be no misunderstanding.

Dead, Prayers for

My son has been reading the Bible recently — the Catholic Bible and the King James Version. He doesn't understand about Catholics praying for the dead. Where does the Catholic Church get this belief?

Both from the Bible and from reason, as well as the earliest traditions of the Church (see 2 Maccabees 12:43-46). This passage has considerable dogmatic importance as it testifies a clear belief in personal immortality and the value of intercessory prayer for the dead. This thinking has resulted in today's Jewish Kaddish for the dead. The Church has defined dogma on purgatory and the Communion of Saints from which this teaching flows. I would recommend that your son visit a library and read the article on purgatory in the *New Catholic Encyclopedia*.

Death, Resignation to

I am having a serious operation soon. I keep saying to myself that I don't care if I live or die. My husband expects so much of me and he has no patience. To me life has been a tough go raising a large family. I love them all and they are good to me, but yet I never see them very often. Is it bad to wish to die if you know you have led a good life?

We are all born to die, and death really begins our life. But it is best to leave all in the hands of God. A Christian should have no fear of death and should welcome it in the spirit of St. Francis of Assisi welcoming Sister Death. But the time and manner should be according to the will of God. While it is not wrong to ask God to take you, it is more saintly to say, "Your will be done."

End of World

What is meant by the end of the world? I read an article which says that someday the world will come to an end. I also read that in my Bible. If that is true, please explain why at the end of the glory prayer we say "world without end. Amen."

We are talking about two different "worlds." There is the physical world in which we live and there is the spiritual world of God. The Latin language from which our liturgical prayers come makes a distinction which English does not. The Latin word for the physical world is "*mundus*." In the Gloria the word used is "*secula*" which for want of a better English expression is also translated "world" but means more "an age" or "a time." The word when used in the Gloria refers to the world of God which is without beginning or end. As regards the physical world, the Bible tells us it will come to an end. This does not mean that it will be totally annihilated (although scientists tell us that that this will happen in some billions of years). There will be a destruction of our world as we know it. St. Peter (2 Pet 3:10) says that it will come through fire, adding, "We wait for new heavens and a new earth." We do not know when this will happen, except that Our Lord promised it will come ("You do not know the day or the hour") quickly. Though there will be signs, they will not be easily recognized.

End of World and Jehovah's Witnesses

What will happen to the earth after the end of the world? Will it be destroyed and annihilated? A member of Jehovah's Witnesses claims that at the end of the world the earth will be cleansed by fire and then made into a paradise to be inhabited only by Jehovah's Witnesses. All others will be annihilated and be no more.

We do not know exactly what will happen at the end of the world. Even to say that the world as we know it will end is not to say that it will be annihilated.

The image of fire connected with the day of the Lord is prevalent in both Old and New Testaments. St. Peter (2 Pet 3:12) writes: "The heavens will be destroyed in flames and the elements will melt away in a blaze." However, this is not annihilation because he adds: "What we await are new heavens and a new earth where, according to his promise, the justice of God will reside." Nevertheless, the passage quoted above from Peter is the only scriptural passage which states that a conflagration will destroy the world on that final day. St. Peter's view that there will be a new heaven and a new earth is also found in the prophet Isaiah (Is 65:17, 66:22). The universal salvific will of God is for the salvation of all. Thus, only those who turn away from God through sin will be lost.

Jehovah's Witnesses' beliefs are apocalyptic in nature, depending largely on misinterpretation of the Book of Revelation. The sect appeals only to people of little theological or philosophical background who can accept preposterous doctrines without intellectual qualms or questioning. Converts know little of their own religions. God's redeeming love is a great mystery, but the Scriptures present it as God's gift to mankind, dependent only on our active response to God. We understand the future life poorly because it is reserved in God's mystery, but we know that we will be perfectly happy. Thus the Christian in the Spirit of the Book of Revelation cries out: "Maranatha! Come, Lord Jesus!"

Experimentation and Life

I am in high school and I am interested in becoming a doctor. I would like to know the

Church's position on the following: experiments using animals; the use of cadavers, fetuses in practicing medicine; and the recent experiments changing the DNA genetic code.

Long articles have been written on each of these subjects and in the short space allowed I can only indicate an answer. Since animals were given by God for the use of mankind (Gen 1:28), the Church allows their use in medicine as long as they are not cruelly kept or subject to unnecessary pain.

The Church permits examination and study of dead bodies, as long as the remains are treated with respect and in the end cremated or buried.

Theologians condemn any fetal research which involves deliberately induced abortion, or the use of any technique which destroys fetal life or imperils its survival. Fetal research which involves only a risk is permitted in proportion to the value gained by the fetus.

The Church permits willing the body or its organs to science to aid others. One cannot do anything that would involve grave injury to another, born or unborn, even the incurable.

The discovery of the structure and role of the DNA molecule (deoxyribonucleic acid) is one of the great discoveries of all time, paralleling the discovery of splitting the atom which gave birth to nuclear physics. However, the Church is very cautious on how this knowledge is used and condemns such things as cloning. The use of such knowledge to overcome disease is one thing but genetic engineering is quite another.

Funerals

Many of us have numerous questions concerning funerals. How good it would be if our church bulletins would spell out the rules of Christian burial, costs, and so on. Does a funeral Mass always have to be a High Mass? Isn't it better to have Masses said for me before I die than after? Can Mass be said at the funeral home? I've read that Illinois law says one need not be embalmed if buried within 24 hours. What are your thoughts on funerals?

I agree that it does cost far too much to die these days. Christian practice calls for far simpler funerals than is now the custom. The practice of dressing the body and making it look "alive" is not in Christian tradition. Viewing the body is a throwback to a medieval custom of proving "the king is dead." Christian counsels demand a far simpler and less expensive funeral than most have. Some parishes are bypassing the funeral home with a side chapel or room where the body is wrapped in a sheet and placed in a simple coffin that is never opened. A wake service is held the night before burial, after which the family greets friends. The next morning the Mass of the Resurrection is said with a procession to the cemetery and burial.

Embalming has no Christian necessity. In most of the world, Catholics are not embalmed. Usually they are buried on the day of death or the following day. In many countries, by law, the body cannot be brought into the church but must be left in the doorway or vestibule. Often the body is buried and the Mass of Resurrection said later. Anyone who desires that a funeral should follow his or her own preferences should make all arrangements ahead of time. A High Mass is not necessary.

Funerals, White Vestments at

Why does the Church use white vestments at a funeral Mass? I thought white was the color of joy. A funeral is certainly not a happy occasion.

In the revised liturgy following Vatican Council II, the Church sought to emphasize the deeper meaning of death and the funeral. The Mass is now called the Mass of the Resurrection and it is one of joy at the soul being united with its Maker in full happiness and blessedness. Naturally, there is a human sorrow at the passing of a relative or friend because of the separation and sense of loss, but it is the Church's intention to make us all aware that death is not an end, but a beginning. It is to reach that beginning that we are even born. While there is the sorrow of earth, there is also the joy of heaven.

Heaven

We hear so much about heaven and how beautiful it is. Is heaven more beautiful and better than life on earth? Does the Bible say much about it?

The Bible frequently speaks of heaven, in fact the word appears more than 500 times. It is used to mean the place of the redeemed after death, the place where God dwells, and the firmament. Heaven is beyond any adequate description. St. Paul, paraphrasing the Prophet Isaiah writes (1 Cor 2:9): "Eye has not seen, ear has not heard, nor has it so much as dawned on man what God has prepared for those who love him." The peace, happiness and beauty of heaven are beyond imagination. In heaven we will have perfect happiness. Jesus promised that our reward would be great there. In heaven there will be no tears, no pain, no suffering, but joy forever. In heaven we will be joined by those we love and be in the company of saints and angels. Heaven is the place to which we were destined by our creation, which was lost through the sin of Adam, but restored to us through Jesus Christ.

Heaven and Masses

I have heard little or read little about heaven since my Baltimore Catechism days. Have the Church's ideas on purgatory changed since Vatican Council II? Could it be that our trials and pains here on earth are our purgatory? My dad passed away and he was a good man; can I now assume he is in heaven? If so, what good is having Masses said for his soul?

Although Vatican Council II spoke about death and our life with God after death, it did not consider purgatory as such. The Church's teaching on purgatory is not rooted in revelation but logic. The Apostolic Fathers taught the doctrine and also that the faithful departed can be helped by the prayers of the faithful, particularly by the Sacrifice of the Mass. You can hope and even expect that your father is in heaven but you cannot assume the fact since that would be presumption. We do know that God is a Father who shows mercy as well as justice. Since we cannot assume anyone is in heaven (except saints declared as saints by the Church only after miracles and a long canonical procedure), we pray for our dead and offer Mass for them, believing that if the object of our prayers is in heaven God will use those merits gained for someone else. Since your father was a good man, place your trust in God and look forward to being reunited with your father in heaven. Read 2 Maccabees 12:43-46.

Heaven, Location of

In school we are talking about heaven and I asked the teacher: "Where is heaven?" She did not answer me. Will you?

That is a difficult question to answer because we continually think of heaven as a place when it is not so much a place as a state of happiness. It is a state in which we will see and enjoy God. Since God is everywhere, we might say heaven is everywhere. Our difficulty is due to the fact that we live in a world made up of matter and our thinking is concerned with material things and material terms which do not apply to the world of the spirit. God has given us a road map to heaven in the Bible and the Church; for the rest we simply have to trust in Him.

Indulgences

Are plenary and partial indulgences obsolete? We asked a couple of priests and they didn't know under what conditions indulgences are gained.

Pope Paul VI, on January 1, 1967, issued an apostolic constitution, *The Doctrine and Practice of Indulgences.* This was further developed in the *Enchiridion Indulgentiarum* of 1968. These documents reaffirmed the right of the Church to grant indulgences based on the merits of Christ, the merits of the saints, the Power of the Keys, and the doctrine of the Communion of Saints. The main change was the removal of years and days from partial indulgences. This leaves the remission of temporal punishment to the justice of God. The usual conditions for gaining an indulgence are kept. Plenary indulgences are granted for such devotional practices as adoration of the Blessed Sacrament for at least a half hour, devout reading of Scripture for at least a half hour, praying the Rosary, and praying the Way of the Cross. Only one plenary indulgence can be gained in a single day.

Limbo

Please reply to the statement that the Church never did take an official position on limbo when the Baltimore Catechism stated that limbo was a place that unbaptized persons went upon death. Limbo, states the catechism, is just like heaven except that a person will never see God.

Limbo is the name given the place where the dead go who are not in heaven, hell or purgatory. Neither revelation nor the earliest Christian tradition treats this subject. St. Augustine put forth the belief that children who die without baptism are condemned to the real (but mitigated) pains of hell. This teaching was tempered by St. Anselm of Canterbury and after him the Scholastics to the effect that although such children were deprived of eternal beatitude, they existed in a place or state of their own, namely limbo (the edge). The Baltimore Catechism follows this opinion.

The Church has never defined this matter nor has a

conclusion on it come from any council. The nearest to it came in a letter to the Armenians (1321) wherein it was stated: "It (the Roman Church) teaches. . . that the souls. . . of those who die in mortal sin, or with only original sin, descend immediately into hell; however, to be punished with different penalties and in different places." The matter is still discussed and argued today. However, catechesis over the centuries and substantial theological tradition have posited a place called limbo and weight has to be given to this history. While there is no definite doctrine of faith in this matter, parents who lose children before baptism should be encouraged to put their trust in a loving God who wishes salvation for all and whose grace knows no limits.

Rapture

Some Protestant friends told me that if the world ended tomorrow, they would not die but be seized into the air to join the angels. The implication was this would not happen to me. Do you know what they were talking about?

They are speaking of what fundamental Protestants call the "rapture." Their idea comes from a literal interpretation of a verse from St. Paul's Epistle to the Thessalonians (1 Thess 4:17). St. Paul is speaking of the Second Coming of Christ and the resurrection. He describes how the dead will arise first and then adds: "Then we, the living, the survivors, will be caught up with them in the clouds to meet the Lord in the air. . . ." One must be careful in understanding apocalyptic literature; most of the time it is not to be taken literally. Later, Paul himself warns against this

(2 Thess 2:1-2). At this time in his writing Paul was expecting the Second Coming to take place shortly (verse 15) and thus his expression "we the living." Since we know St. Paul died, we cannot take "we the living" literally since in the "we" Paul includes himself. If we cannot take it literally in one place, why should we insist on a literal interpretation in another? If Christ is to come as a thief in the night (1 Thess 5:2), how can He also come with sounding trumpet (1 Thess 4:16)? Proper understanding of the Bible involves the writer's intention and not always his literal expression.

Reincarnation

I read that a soul must be purified of all sins in order to be "reborn." Does that mean that reincarnation really exists?

Certainly not. We are born in the sin of Adam and reborn in the Holy Spirit through baptism. In another sense we are reborn through the Sacrament of Penance, rising anew from the death of sin. This rebirth has nothing to do with reincarnation which is a contradiction of Catholic doctrine. St. Paul (Heb 9:27) tells us "men die only once, and after that comes judgment." In our resurrection we will be united with our bodies, not a series of bodies and personalities.

Resuscitation

What is the Church's teaching regarding cardiopulmonary resuscitation efforts and is this not a threat to dying with dignity? This has been on our minds since we faced a life-saving situation which turned out to be fruitless since the person died. Also, what do moral theologians teach about the length of time the soul remains in the body after death? Is it true that in sudden death the soul may remain longer than in death from a long illness?

I don't like to use the term "dying with dignity" because it is a popularized slogan of euthanasia proponents to permit the terminally ill to commit suicide.

CPR (cardiopulmonary resuscitation) is a standard technique of emergency medical services to restore heartbeat and breathing to victims of heart attacks, drownings and electrical shock. It is the teaching of moral theologians that we must use ordinary means to preserve life. Ordinary means would include normal medical attention, food, drink, medicines, treatments and operations. CPR is considered a standard or normal technique to restore life; so too would be temporary use of oxygen and intravenous feeding; blood transfusions are considered ordinary treatment. CPR has become a very successful form of prompt treatment for certain cases. CPR may be fruitless in the end but we are bound to try it when it is available.

Because of the uncertainty of the moment of death, most theologians allow the administration of the Sacrament of Anointing up to a half hour after apparent death; however, the sacrament can only be given conditionally. There is no distinction between a long and sudden illness.

Salvation

Reading a few Catholic books, I read that being born again is the only way to salvation and heaven. I always thought that salvation and heaven involved keeping the commandments; believing in Jesus; going to church, and being a very good Christian. Are these books right?

You are both correct. When Nicodemus came to see Jesus and talked about salvation (Jn 3), Jesus told him he had to be born again. When Nicodemus asked how this was possible, Jesus replied: "No one can enter into God's kingdom without being begotten of water and Spirit." The Church has always held this to mean the necessity of baptism for salvation. Through baptism, we are born again spiritually into Christ. For one past the age of reason, however, baptism is not enough. We must also keep God's commandments. As St. John also tells us (1 Jn 3:18-23), God rewards because we keep His commandments and live the kind of life He wants. His commandments are these: that we "believe in the name of his Son, Jesus Christ, and we are to love one another as he commanded us." So for salvation we must be born again through baptism and then live the law of the Lord.

Salvation of Jews

Recently my husband's friends and I had a discussion on the Jews. They said Jews cannot go to heaven. I had never heard this before as I was raised to believe that anyone who believes in God and lived by his or her faith could go to heaven and that God was the final judge. They totally disagreed with this and said the Jews must believe in Jesus Christ as their Savior. Can Jews go to heaven?

The Church teaches us that Jews, Moslems and even pagans can be saved because Jesus Christ died for the redemption of all. In its *Dogmatic Constitution on the Church*, Vatican Council II taught: "Basing itself on Scripture and Tradition, it teaches that the Church, a pilgrim now on earth, is necessary for salvation: the one Christ is mediator and the way of salvation. . . . He himself explicitly asserted the necessity of faith and baptism (compare Mk, 16:16, Jn 3:5)." Having said this the Council points out that there are various ways one can be joined to the Church, considering Protestants who accept the Gospel; Jews who are people of the covenant; Moslems, who profess the faith of Abraham, and acknowledge the one true God. As for pagans, the Council declared: "Those, who through no fault of their own, do not know the Gospel of Christ or His Church, but who nevertheless seek God with a sincere heart, try in their actions to do His will as they know it through the dictates of their conscience — those too may achieve eternal salvation."

Your friends are limiting the mercy and justice of God.

Salvation Justified by Faith

I cannot understand why Catholics reject the teaching that salvation is justified by faith. After all, it is what a man believes that determines his judgment.

The doctrine that man is justified and saved by faith alone is the invention of Martin Luther and became a plank of the Reformation. The Church has always held that *faith and good works* are necessary for salvation. The reasons for Luther's advocacy of this teaching are rooted in his own personality. He misinterpreted St. Paul in Paul's Letter to the Romans (3:28).

Actually, if you are proposing this doctrine as a rule of faith, you are even out of step with most Protestant churches which over the years have come to reject it, and have returned to the original Catholic position that good deeds are also necessary for salvation.

Salvation of Protestants

My mother is Protestant and my father is Catholic. My brother and I are Catholics. I would like to know: since mother is not of the Catholic faith will she still go to heaven? She has been going to Sunday Mass with us for 16 years although she does not receive Communion. How does the Church view this, and will it be a sin against her in any way?

Of course your mother can go to heaven. Anyone who follows his or her conscience and tries to do the will of God as it is known to him can go to heaven. If your mother has been going to church with you every Sunday for 16 years, I suggest that you invite her to become a Catholic. Then the family can be united in the Eucharist.

I have a friend who, although a Protestant, accompanied his family to church for 20 years. One Saturday he was standing outside church while his wife was inside going to confession. One of the priests came out, said hello, and remarked, "Dick, I've seen you in church for years. Why haven't you become a Catholic?" My friend replied, "No one has ever asked me."

The priest asked him and the entire family was most happily surprised when dad went to Holy Communion that Easter.

Perhaps your mother just needs an invitation. But even if she doesn't feel she is called to be a Catholic, God takes everything into consideration and judges each person on the individual conscience. Faith is after all a free gift of God.

Salvation Only in the Church

I am puzzled over a statement credited to the writings of Vatican Council II which states: "Whosoever, therefore, knowing that the Catholic Church was made necessary by God through Jesus Christ, would refuse to enter her or remain in her could not be saved." I have known several non-Catholics who have taken instructions and not entered the Church. I also have several non-Catholic relatives and friends who I feel are very fine Christians. Am I misinterpreting the meaning of this statement?

The quotation that puzzles you is from the *Decree on Missionary Activity*. It is another way of stating the old saying, "Outside the Church, no salvation." However, this must be understood.

What it means is that if a person knowing the Catholic Church to be the true Church rejects that Church, then that person cannot be saved.

Non-Catholics who have taken instructions and not entered the Church usually do so because they are not convinced that the Catholic Church is the true Church. They are in non-culpable ignorance. This is also true of non-Catholics who believe their own religion to be true. In both cases these people are following their consciences and are doing God's will as they understand it.

The important words in your quotation are "knowing that the Catholic Church was made necessary by God." If a person knows this and rejects the Church, God rejects that person. If people (such as Protestants or pagans), however, do not know this fact, God then judges them on how they respond to their own consciences, even though from a Catholic viewpoint those consciences may be wrong.

Sheol

I am teaching my children the Rosary. One of them questions the Apostles' Creed where it says: "He descended into hell." I always accepted this as part of my Catholic upbringing. Since Christ was sinless, why would He have died and gone to hell?

The phrase you mentioned has to be interpreted with 1 Peter 3:19 and 4:6 in mind. The Jewish word for hell is *sheol*, which means the abode of the dead and not necessarily the place of punishment of the fallen angels and sinful humans. The generally accepted interpretation is that after death Christ went to *sheol* to lead into heaven those who had died in favor with God but who could not enter heaven until Christ reopened it by His redemption.

Another interpretation is that on His way to heaven Christ paused to proclaim to the fallen angels His triumphal victory through the Cross and to confirm for all time their condemnation because of sin. However, the first interpretation is the one accepted by most commentators. Newer translations of the Bible avoid use of the word "hell" when *sheol* is meant.

Suicide

How does God deal with people who kill themselves? What does the Bible have to say about suicide? Is one who kills himself judged the same as if he murdered someone else?

I cannot answer your first question. God judges each person on an individual basis and on facts known only to Him. Suicide is a violation of the Fifth Commandment: Thou shall not kill. Vatican Council II in its *Constitution on the Church in the Modern World* ruled: "Whatever is opposed to life itself, such as any type of murder, genocide, abortion, euthanasia, and willful self destruction. . . . all these things and others of their like are infamies indeed. They poison human society, they do more harm to those who do them than to those who suffer the injury. Moreover, they are a supreme dishonor to the Creator."

Life is a gift of God and only He has dominion over it. From the moment of conception life must be guarded with the greatest care. A person who commits suicide dies rejecting God's dominion and this is the sin of final impenitence. However, having said all that, we must still exercise great care in making individual judgments. Since suicide is an unnatural act, against human instincts, many theologians hold that most people who commit suicide are not in full possession of their faculties. Acute depression can distort reality, clouding one's judgment and limiting rational thinking. In cases of doubt, the Church permits ecclesiastical burial, leaving final judgment to the justice of God.

Unforgivable Sin

I read that Jesus said there is a sin which cannot be forgiven. I have committed many sins and I wonder if I have committed an unforgivable sin. I would like to stop worrying.

The only unforgivable sin is the sin against the Holy Spirit which the Church teaches is final impenitence. According to Matthew's Gospel, any sin that can be repented can be forgiven (12:31-32). The Spirit continually calls the sinner to repentance. When a sinner rejects this call to repentance and dies in his or her sin, that person dies rejecting the Holy Spirit, or God. Since sins cannot be repented after death such a person dies in a sin that is unforgivable; that is, he or she dies rejecting God and remains in that state.

Vision of God

Among other strange statements in the Bible, I find the following: "Moses went up with Aaron, Nadab and Abihu, and seventy elders of Israel. They saw the God of Israel beneath whose feet there was, it seemed, a sapphire pavement pure as the heavens themselves" (Ex 24:9-10). How does one reconcile this passage with St. John's "No one has ever seen God" (Jn 1:18 and 1 Jn 3:12)?

There is a standard Old Testament axiom that no one can see God and live (Deut 18:16). This has a reflection in the quotation from John. The idea of the Israelites that death would follow seeing God was based not on His invisibility but on His sanctity and that anyone who violated this was subject to death (see 2 Sam

6:7 and Judges 6:23, 13:22). God being pure spirit cannot be seen, but He did make His presence known (thunder, lightning, a cloud, a burning bush). Moses and his companions had some kind of an apparition of God in which they experienced the presence of God, but they did not see Him in the literal sense. God was so sacred to the Israelites that His name was not even mentioned by the people.

Bibliography

Kübler-Ross, Elisabeth. *Living with Death and Dying.*

Kübler-Ross, Elisabeth, and Mal Warshaw. *To Live Until We Say Good-bye.*

Consumer Reports, Ed. *Funerals: Consumers' Last Rights.*

Draznin, Yaffa. *How to Prepare for Death: Your Own or Someone Else's.*

Kübler-Ross, Elisabeth. *Questions and Answers on Death and Dying.*

Kübler-Ross, Elisabeth. *On Death and Dying.*

Nowell, Robert. *What a Modern Catholic Believes About Death.*

Shea, John. *Sin, Heaven and Hell.*

Hardon, John A., S.J. *Catholic Catechism.*

Lawler, R., et al. *The Teaching of Christ.*

Brown, Raymond E., S.S., et al. *Jerome Biblical Commentary.*

Fuller, Reginald C., Ed. *New Catholic Commentary on Holy Scripture.*

Nevins, Albert J., M.M., Ed. *Maryknoll Catholic Dictionary.*

Rahner, Karl, Ed. *Encyclopedia of Theology.*

Tanquerey, A., S.S. *The Spiritual Life.*

Leon-Dufour. *Dictionary of Biblical Theology.*

Brugger-Baker, Eds. *Philosophical Dictionary.*

Aumann, Jordan, O.P. *Spiritual Theology.*

Enchiridion of Indulgences. Catholic Book Publishing Co.

The Rites. Pueblo Publishing Co., Inc.

Denzinger, H. *The Sources of Catholic Dogma.*

McFadden, Charles J., O.S.A. *Medical Ethics.*

McFadden, Charles J., O.S.A. *Challenge to Morality.*

Garrigou-LaGrange, O.P. *Life Everlasting.*

Guardini, R. *The Last Things.*

Schillebeeckx, E.H. *Death of a Christian (Layman in the Church).*

Rahner, Karl. *On the Theology of Death.*

Index

Francis of Assisi, St. 1
Fundamentalism 88, 91, 97
Funeral 134, 135

Glorified body 53, 99ff.
God's presence 51ff.
Greek immortality 26-27
Gregory of Nyssa, St. 72
Gregory, Pope St. 67, 72, 100
Gumpel, Peter 120

Hardon, John, S.J. 33, 66, 103
Heaven 47ff., 135, 136, 137
Heaven, definition of 53
Heaven, nature of 53ff.
Hell 58ff.
Hell, Catholic dogma on 61, 64
Hell, punishment of 63
Hitler, Adolf 7
Hinduism and soul 10
Human experimentation 132-133

Ignatius, St. 23, 24
Immortality 19ff., 22
Immortality and St. John 22
Immortality and St. Paul 22
Indulgence 77ff.
Indulgence, conditions for 83-84, 87
Indulgence, definition of 77-78
Indulgence, partial 86-87
Indulgence, plenary 84, 137
Indulgenced acts 84-86
Indulgenced prayers 106ff.
Innocent III 118
Irenaeus, St. 20
Islam and soul 9, 20

Jansenists 118
Jarrett, Bede 59, 95
Jehovah's Witnesses 88-89, 131

Origen 64, 65

Paleolithic death customs 8
Parousia 90ff., 96ff.
Paul, St. 3, 4, 22, 28, 29, 30, 49, 54, 90, 94, 98, 99
Paul VI 6, 78, 82
Pesch, Rudolf 92
Peter Pan 1
Pharisees and afterlife 17
Pius VI 119
Pius XII 53
Plenary indulgence at death 45
Polycarp, St. 23ff.
Power of Keys 80, 81, 119
Prayers for the dead 129
Purgatory 68ff.
Purgatory and Scripture 69, 70
Purgatory, doctrine of 68
Purgatory, modern thinking on 74
Purgatory, nature of 73

Rahner, Karl 27-28, 53, 61, 63, 90-91, 92, 93
Rapture 88, 97, 139
Ratzinger, Joseph 27, 62
Reformed Judaism 18
Reincarnation 10, 140
Resuscitation 34ff., 38, 140
Resurrected body 99-100
Resurrection 26ff., 98ff.
Resurrection in Paul 29, 30
Resurrection of Christ 28-29
Resurrection vs. immortality 26ff.

Sabom, Michael B. 35-36
Sadducees and afterlife 17
Salvation 141-142
Salvation of Jews 142-143
Salvation of Protestants 144
Salvation only in Church 145
Santayana, George 4, 6

Sartre, Jean Paul 60
Satan as antichrist 93
Science and immortality 19
Second Coming 97, 98
Shaw, George Bernard 60
Shea, John 47, 58
Sheol 13ff., 27, 59, 60, 117, 146
Sin against Holy Ghost 64
Snite, Fred 38
Socrates 1
Soul 6, 10, 11, 14-15
Suicide 147
Survivors of dead 41

Teaching of Christ 32, 67, 94
Tertullian 72
Tests for death 38-39
Tetzel, John 77
Thomas à Kempis 5
Thompson, Francis 54
Tradition 70-71
Treasury of Church 79-80, 81
Twain, Mark 7

Vespasian 5
Vigilius, Pope 64
Vision of God 148

Warshaw, Mal 41
White, Ellen 88
Wright, Cardinal John 42